contents

getting started

WE all have to eat and, eventually, you'll probably have to cook to feed yourself. Now, when you have the family kitchen and a helpful adult around 24/7, is the perfect time to learn about food and how to cook. We bet it won't take long for you to discover that cooking is a lot more than just making food to eat: it's heaps of fun, and creative and exciting, too.

Here are some basic tips for getting it right in the kitchen: even your mum and dad and professional chefs stick to simple safety and hygiene guidelines like these.

before you start

Make sure you've got the okay from an adult to use the kitchen before you start anything, and ask someone to hang around the first few times you make something. Even professional cooks don't know everything, and they all have assistants, so never be afraid to ask an adult to explain a recipe to you or for help in doing something.

understand the recipe

Read the recipe through a few times before you start preparing. Make sure you know when you have to start cooking, what ingredients and utensils you need, and if something in the menu needs to be made a day ahead.

defrosting meat

Always thaw meat, seafood and poultry, covered, in the refrigerator. In a pinch, you can defrost these items in your microwave oven, but take care because some outside edges of the meat can actually cook. Place meat on a tray in the refrigerator as it defrosts to stop it dripping onto other food.

keep your hair out of the food

Tie long hair back from your face to keep it from falling into the food or onto food preparation surfaces. It will also keep you from singeing any wayward strands. Now you know why most chefs wear hats.

personal hygiene

Don't touch your hair or mouth, or leave the kitchen to do something else, without washing your hands again before touching any food. Stay out of the kitchen if you're sick.

clean hands

Always wash your hands with soap and warm water (don't forget your fingernails), and dry them on a clean towel or absorbent paper. This is extremely important if you're handling uncooked food. Before making sandwiches, cutting fruit or tossing salads, always wash your hands thoroughly. If you have a cut on your hand, wear disposable gloves. Always wash your hands after touching any uncooked meat, seafood or poultry.

clothing

Wear short-sleeved or tight-fitting long-sleeved tops. Loose-fitting ones can drop into the food, or worse, catch fire over a hot stove.

watch your feet

Wear closed-toed shoes when cooking (more than one chef has dropped a sharp knife, point-first, onto his or her toes). It's not a bad idea to wear non-slip shoes as well.

tidy up as you go

Keep the worktop and the rest of the preparation area clean and tidy as you work. Wipe up any spills or grease spots that occur during cooking as you go. Never use the same cloth for wiping up spills, for your hands or for the kitchen worktop. Rinse the cloth or sponge you use constantly in hot soapy water. And if you wash any equipment you've used, or at least rinse it well, you can use it again for the next thing you're going to make. Even if you don't use it again, at least the cooked food won't have been able to cement itself to the bottom of the pans while you're eating.

taste as you go

It's a good idea to taste food as you prepare it, to test for flavour, but don't taste from the stirring spoon or salad fork then return it into the saucepan or serving bowl; use different, clean fresh cutlery every time you taste. And don't add salt to enhance the flavour: your idea of perfect seasoning may be far too much for someone else.

put stuff away

Put the food you've finished with back in the refrigerator or pantry, checking first to make certain that the lids are on tight. If you're putting away any uncooked meat, seafood or poultry, make sure it's enclosed tightly in cling film or a snap-lock bag, or sealed tightly in a storage container. Ditto with raw vegetables: wrap them tightly and return them to the crisper in the fridge.

kitchen equipment

knives
Choosing the right knife for the right job is something you'll learn over time. Most cooks use only four or five different knives; ask the main cook in your family for advice as well as some vital safety tips.

grater
Used for shredding vegetables, cheese and, if you haven't got a crusher, garlic (using the smallest holes). Take care that you don't grate your knuckles or fingertips on the razor-sharp holes.

saucepans
Come in many shapes and sizes and, like knives, each pan has a different purpose, capacity being just one. Make sure you turn a pan's handles away from the stove's front to avoid knocking the pan onto the floor.

whisks
The best tool for beating or whipping air into egg whites or cream, to stiffen or increase them in volume, is a whisk. You'll have to learn how to rotate your wrist to whisk well, but it's not difficult.

chopping boards
Whether it's plastic or wood, your chopping board must be kept really clean. Try keeping different coloured boards for different foods: red for raw meat; yellow for bread; and green for vegetables and fruit.

measuring spoons
Sold as sets which measure from 1 tablespoon for the largest down to ⅛ teaspoon for the smallest, they measure both dry and liquid ingredients. Level the top flat with the back of a knife for accuracy with dry ingredients.

measuring cups
These come in sets, too, usually sized to measure 1, ½, ⅓ and ¼ cups. Spoon dry ingredients into the cup then drag the back of a knife across the surface to level the top of the cup's content.

kitchen scales
For measuring foods (like whole fruits or spaghetti) that can't be squeezed into a measuring cup, or when needing an exact weight for flour or sugar when baking, use your kitchen scales.

measuring jugs
These have millilitre and pint measurements written down the side. To measure precisely, place on a level surface and pour in an approximate amount of liquid. Face the jug at eye level and check the quantity for accuracy.

melon baller
You'll find many uses for this tool besides scooping out melon (potato, butter and ice-cream, too) balls: for instance, coring apples and pears, or scraped down the side of chocolate to make long curls.

vegetable peelers

Not only do these peel potatoes, apples and the like, they also slice carrots, or cucumber into super-fine ribbons for salads, and potato into thin enough slices to fry for homemade chips.

oven mitts

Oven mitts or pot holders protect your fingers from being burned by escaping steam from a lifted lid or when pouring hot liquid, as well as the obvious — taking hot dishes out of the oven or microwave.

pastry brushes

Flat wood brushes, with either natural or plastic bristles, are used for greasing oven trays and cake pans; brushing water or milk on the edges of pastry parcels to seal them; or to brush a marinade onto food.

wooden spoons

A favourite tool of many cooks, wooden spoons are great to stir with because they don't scratch non-stick surfaces and are comfortable in your hand. Make sure to wash and dry thoroughly after use.

spatulas

These long-handled utensils have flat plastic or rubber, or even wood or metal ends, perfect for scraping cake batter from a bowl or folding whipped or beaten food into a mixture without deflating it.

skewers

Vegetables, meat, seafood and poultry can be threaded onto skewers for grilling. If you use wooden or bamboo skewers, soak them in water for an hour before using so they don't splinter or scorch.

electrical appliances

A toaster, kettle or any electrical appliance is easy enough to use, but remember to unplug them when you've finished and before cleaning them. Remember to never leave the kitchen with any electrical appliance operating.

microplane grater

The microplane is a new version of a traditional zester. It looks like a small metal cricket bat covered with sharp tiny holes. It can be used to grate rind, chocolate, cheese, garlic or ginger.

cutters

There are dozens of cutter sizes and designs; use them to cut out biscuits or shapes from rolled-out dough to top a pie. They make good templates to fill with sprinkles or icing sugar on cake tops.

sieves

These are used to shake sifted dry ingredients like icing sugar over the top of a cake or to drain cooked pasta or vegies. Strain your fresh juice into a glass to capture the pips and pulp.

how do you do it?

◀ **remove bacon rind**
When chopping bacon, it's a good idea to cut away the hard outside rind first. Place the rashers on a chopping board; using a sharp knife, cut through fat as close to rind as possible along the length of the rasher. Scissors can also be used to do this job neatly.

◀ **chop onions finely**
Cut the top end from an onion then slice the onion in half lengthways; discard skin from both halves. Slice each half thinly, first lengthways then widthways. Throw away the onion root end and green core.

◀ **crush and peel garlic**
Separate, but do not peel, garlic cloves from the bulb; place on a chopping board then use the flat side of a heavy knife to press down firmly on each clove. As the clove is flattened, the skin splits and will be easy to pull off. Next, crush or chop the garlic according to how you want it.

◄ prepare peppers

Hold the pepper stem in one hand then slice lengthways into quarters with a sharp knife. Discard the stem and seed core. Flatten quarters, skin-side down, on a chopping board; run the knife flat across each piece to remove membrane and remaining seeds.

◄ deseed tomatoes

Some recipes, salsa, for example, call for deseeded tomatoes, usually so that the final mixture won't be too watery. First, cut the tomato in half lengthways then use a teaspoon to scoop out the seeds and pulp (if you want to keep these for another use, scoop them into a bowl).

◄ roast peppers

Place prepared pepper quarters, skin-side up, on oven tray under heated grill or in very hot oven until the skin blisters and blackens. Place pepper pieces in an airtight paper or plastic bag for 10 minutes then peel the skin away carefully.

◄ peel a tomato

Cut a shallow cross in the base of the tomato. Place the tomato in a heatproof bowl; cover with boiling water, stand 2 minutes then cover tomato with cold water to cool. Use your fingers to peel away the skin; starting from the cross end, pull towards the top.

◄ separate lettuce leaves

With the cored-end facing down, smash lettuce hard onto the worktop. This will loosen the outer leaves, which will then come away easily. Holding the cored end under cold running water will also force the outer leaves to fall off intact.

◄ slice and pit an avocado

Use a small knife to make several lengthways cuts around the avocado, through to the stone. Use your fingers to pull away the strips of peel, from stem-end downward, then use the knife to lever out the slices, one at a time. To pit an avocado, cut the avocado in half lengthways around the stone. Twist halves in different directions. Use a spoon to scoop out the stone.

◄ **separate an egg**

Crack an egg gently over a small bowl with the back of a knife. Transfer the yolk from half-shell to half-shell until all the white drops into the bowl. Another method is to crack an egg into a small shallow bowl or saucer, cover the yolk with a glass then tilt the saucer carefully so that the white runs into a separate bowl.

◄ **melt chocolate**

Break up the chocolate pieces into a microwave-safe bowl; place in microwave oven on MEDIUM (55%) for 1 minute for every 200g of chocolate. Take the bowl out of the microwave using oven mitts and stir the chocolate. If it hasn't melted completely, repeat the microwave oven melting method, in shorter bursts, until chocolate is smooth

◄ **make strawberry fans**

Make four or five vertical cuts into a strawberry from the tip end, being careful not to cut all the way through. Gently spread the slices into a fan shape to decorate ice-creams or cakes, or to hang over the rim of a juice or smoothie glass.

juice a lemon

To get as much juice from a lemon as possible, place it in a microwave oven on HIGH (100%) for 30 seconds, or cover it with hot water for about a minute. Next, roll it, pressing firmly, along your kitchen bench, to break up the pulp and release more juice.

test if a cake is done

Push a metal skewer into the highest part of the cake. You can use a wooden one, but it's easier to tell if there's cake mixture stuck on a metal skewer. Pull the skewer out, and if no cake mixture sticks to it, the cake is cooked.

◀ grate lemon rind

Use a citrus zester (or microplane if you have one) or the smallest holes on a four-sided grater. Carefully grate the rind onto a piece of baking parchment; it will slide easily off the paper. Don't press down too hard on the lemon because you only want to grate the outer yellow rind. Always grate a lemon before you juice it.

◀ turn out a cake

Using tea-towels or oven mitts, remove the cake tin from the oven and sit tin on a wooden board. Turn the cake upside-down onto a wire rack; remove tin then the lining paper. Put another rack over cake bottom and, holding the two racks like a sandwich, turn the cake over so it now is top-side up.

◀ cut citrus rind strips

If necessary, ask an adult to help you remove the rind from a lemon, orange or lime; cut away any of the bitter white pith that sticks to the rind. Use a sharp knife to cut the rind into really thin strips to sprinkle over salads or desserts.

◀ roast nuts

Roasting nuts releases their flavour and changes them from soft to crunchy. Spread the quantity of nuts you're using in a single layer onto a baking tray then roast in a preheated moderate oven for about 5 minutes. You can also stir the nuts in a dry frying pan over medium heat until they are lightly browned and fragrant.

drinks
and shakes

For the very best results, make your drink or shake just before you want to serve it. If you keep juices, they can sometimes separate whilst they are standing. They may also lose some of their essential vitamins and minerals: fresh drinks and smoothies retain their goodness to give you maximum benefit!

did you know?

smoothie
A smoothie is a combination of fruit and dairy products, such as milk, ice-cream or yogurt, that is blended until thick and smooth.

frappé
A frappé is a frozen flavoured liquid (usually a blend of whole fruit – mangoes, pineapple, etc – or fruit juice with crushed ice) that has a slushy consistency.

strawberry milkshake

preparation time 5 minutes   **makes** 1 litre (4 cups)

250g strawberries, chopped coarsely
2 cups (500ml) milk
2 scoops strawberry ice-cream
½ cup (125ml) strawberry-flavoured topping

1 Blend or process all ingredients until smooth.

chocolate malted
milkshake

preparation time 5 minutes **makes** 1 litre (4 cups)

⅓ cup (40g) malted milk powder
⅓ cup (80ml) chocolate-flavoured topping
1 cup (250ml) chocolate ice-cream
2½ cups (625ml) milk

1 Blend or process all ingredients until smooth.

tip Ask an adult to show you how to properly use a blender or food processor for your first few attempts.

milkshakes, frappés and frosty fruit drinks

raspberry cordial

preparation time 15 minutes (plus refrigeration time) **cooking time** 10 minutes **makes** 750ml

1 Blend 300g thawed frozen raspberries and ½ cup (125ml) cranberry juice until smooth.

2 Combine 2 cups (500ml) water and 1 cup (220g) caster sugar in medium saucepan, stir over heat, without boiling, until sugar dissolves; bring to a boil. Reduce heat; simmer, without stirring, 5 minutes. Add raspberry mixture to pan; bring to a boil. Reduce heat; simmer, uncovered, 2 minutes.

3 Strain cordial into medium jug, discard seeds; refrigerate 30 minutes. Mix one part cordial to three parts chilled water or soda water. Cordial will keep, covered in a sterilised bottle, in the refrigerator for up to 2 weeks.

tropical punch

preparation time 15 minutes (plus refrigeration time) **makes** 2.5 litres (10 cups)

You need half a medium pineapple weighing approximately 650g for this recipe.

1 Strain 425g can sliced mango in natural juice over small bowl; reserve juice. Chop mango slices finely; combine mango and reserved juice in large bowl with 3 cups (750ml) tropical fruit juice.

2 Stir in 300g finely chopped pineapple, 250g finely chopped strawberries, 2 tablespoons finely shredded fresh mint, 1 tablespoon caster sugar and 3 cups (750ml) ginger ale.

3 Refrigerate punch 2 hours before serving.

tropical frappé

preparation time 5 minutes **makes** 1 litre (4 cups)

1 Blend or process 1 cup (250ml) passionfruit sorbet, 1 cup (250ml) orange juice, 450g can crushed pineapple and one medium banana until combined.

tips Refrigerate all ingredients before making these juice drinks. ★ Serve the drinks within 30 minutes of making.

pineapple juice with watermelon ice

preparation time 10 minutes (plus freezing time) **makes** 1.25 litres (5 cups)

You need a 550g piece of watermelon and half a large pineapple weighing approximately 1kg for this recipe.

1 Blend or process 280g coarsely chopped seedless watermelon until smooth. Using back of large spoon, push through sieve; discard solids. Pour juice into ice-cube tray; freeze until set.

2 Push 650g coarsely chopped pineapple and four peeled large oranges through juice extractor.

3 Divide juice among glasses; top with watermelon ice-cubes.

mandarin apple juice with passionfruit ice

preparation time 10 minutes (plus freezing time) **makes** 1.25 litres (5 cups)

1 Using fork, combine the pulp of three passionfruit and ⅓ cup (80ml) cold water in small bowl. Pour passionfruit mixture into ice-cube tray; freeze until set.

2 Push six coarsely chopped large apples and six medium mandarins through juice extractor.

3 Divide juice among serving glasses; top with passionfruit ice-cubes.

berry frappé

preparation time 5 minutes **makes** 1 litre (4 cups)

1 Blend or process 1 cup (250ml) mixed berry sorbet, 2 cups (500ml) cranberry juice and 1 cup (150g) frozen mixed berries until combined.

tips Experiment with different combinations of berries in this frappé – strawberries, blackberries, blueberries and raspberries are all delicious options.

fruit tango smoothie

preparation time 10 minutes **makes** 4 cups

1 medium mango
1 medium banana
2 strawberries
200g tub honey and vanilla yogurt
1 cup milk
10 ice cubes
2 teaspoons honey
1 scoop vanilla ice-cream
2 passionfruit

1 On a chopping board, cut the cheeks from the mango.

2 Cut the flesh from around the mango stone.

3 Using a spoon, scoop the flesh from the mango cheeks. Chop the banana and cut the tops off the strawberries. Put the mango, banana, strawberries, yogurt, milk, ice, honey and ice-cream in the blender, put the lid on, and blend until the mixture is smooth. Remove the lid. Turn the power off.

4 Cut the passionfruit in half. Using a small spoon, scoop out the passionfruit pulp, add it to the smoothie, and stir until mixed together.

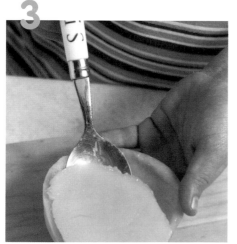

tip Many different fruits can be used in smoothies: use what's in season — that's when it's at its best and cheapest.

malted banana smoothie

preparation time 5 minutes makes 3 cups

2 medium bananas
1 cup milk
¼ cup malted milk powder
1 tablespoon honey
8 ice cubes
1 scoop vanilla ice-cream

1 Cut up the bananas on a chopping board.

2 Put all the ingredients into a blender, put the lid on then blend until the mixture is smooth.

tip The flavour of your smoothie will change with the ripeness of the fruit. Use overripe bananas for a sweeter taste.

orange and ginger juice

preparation time 15 minutes cooking time 15 minutes serves 4

8 medium oranges (2kg)
6cm piece fresh ginger (30g), grated

1 Juice oranges on citrus squeezer; discard seeds. Stir in ginger.

2 Pour into four serving glasses.

pineapple, orange and strawberry juice

preparation time 10 minutes serves 1

1 small orange (180g), peeled, quartered
150g pineapple, chopped coarsely
2 strawberries
¼ cup (60ml) water

1 Push orange, pineapple and strawberries through juice extractor into glass; stir in the water.

watermelon juice

preparation time 5 minutes serves 1

450g watermelon, seeds removed, chopped coarsely
4 fresh mint leaves

1 Blend or process all ingredients until smooth; pour into glass.

tips Refrigerate all ingredients before making these juice drinks.
★ Serve the drinks within 30 minutes of making.

Eating a good breakfast kick-starts your day, helping you to concentrate better in school. It also gives you plenty of the minerals and vitamins you need to keep going all day.

breakfast

perfect porridge

preparation time 5 minutes cooking time 5 minutes serves 1 or 2

1⅓ cups water
½ cup rolled oats
milk

1 Put the water and oats in a medium saucepan on the stove, and turn the heat to medium. Stir the mixture with a wooden spoon until it boils.

2 Turn the heat a little lower to stop the porridge boiling over the side of the pan. Stir the porridge for about 4 minutes or until it is thick and creamy. Spoon the porridge into serving bowls and pour over as much milk as you like. Serve with the topping of your choice.

tip Here is a quick way to cook porridge. Mix the oats and water together in a microwave-safe serving bowl. Put the bowl in the microwave oven without a lid and cook on HIGH (100%) for 1 minute. The porridge will puff up – be careful as it will be very hot. Using oven mitts, remove the dish and stir well. Return the dish to the microwave oven and cook the porridge for 1 minute more or until the porridge is thick and creamy.

toppings

cinnamon sugar

Combine 1 teaspoon ground cinnamon with 2 tablespoons caster sugar in small bowl. Sprinkle over bowls of porridge. Any remaining cinnamon sugar can be sprinkled on hot buttered toast for an after-school snack. (Pictured top right.)

apple and pear compote

Peel, core and coarsely chop 1 large apple and 1 medium pear. Combine fruit with ⅓ cup apple juice and 1 tablespoon lemon juice in medium saucepan over medium heat; bring to a boil. Reduce heat; simmer, covered, stirring occasionally, about 15 minutes or until fruit softens and liquid is absorbed. (Pictured middle right.)

honey and yogurt

Divide ⅓ cup (95g) vanilla yogurt and 1 tablespoon honey among bowls of porridge. (Pictured bottom right.)

sweet strawberry

Chop some fresh strawberries. Drizzle some honey over the top of the porridge or sprinkle with brown sugar, and top with strawberries. (Pictured below.)

healthy breakfast bowls

preparation time 20 minutes **serves** 4

⅓ cup (25g) All-Bran
⅓ cup (20g) Special K
⅓ cup (5g) puffed wheat
250g strawberries, hulled
1 cup (280g) vanilla yogurt
⅓ cup (80ml) passionfruit pulp

1 Combine cereals in small bowl.

2 Cut six strawberries in half; reserve. Slice remaining strawberries thinly.

3 Divide half of the cereal mixture among four 250ml serving bowls; divide half of the yogurt, all the strawberry slices and half of the passionfruit pulp among bowls. Continue layering with remaining cereal and yogurt; top with reserved strawberry halves and remaining passionfruit pulp.

pears on fruit toast

preparation time 5 minutes cooking time 3 minutes makes 4

4 slices fruit bread
1 small pear (180g), sliced thinly
2 teaspoons brown sugar

1 Preheat grill.

2 Toast fruit bread.

3 Place pear slices on each slice of toast.

4 Sprinkle pear with sugar. Toast under grill about 2 minutes or until browned lightly.

peach muesli

preparation time 25 minutes (plus refrigeration time) serves 4

2 cups (220g) natural muesli
1⅓ cups (330ml) apple juice
¾ cup (200g) country-style yogurt
1¼ cups (185g) coarsely chopped dried peaches
2 tablespoons honey
¾ cup (180ml) milk
1 large apple (200g), peeled, grated
1 large peach (220g), cut into wedges
¼ cup (20g) toasted shredded coconut

1 Combine muesli, juice, yogurt, dried peach, honey and milk in large bowl. Cover; refrigerate overnight.

2 Stir apple into muesli mixture; serve topped with peach wedges and sprinkled with coconut.

bacon and eggs

preparation time 10 minutes cooking time 10 minutes serves 4

4 rashers thinly-cut bacon (120g), cut in half
2 spring onions, sliced thinly
4 eggs
4 thick slices white bread, toasted

1 Preheat oven to moderately hot (200°C/180°C fan-assisted). Grease four holes of 12-hole (⅓-cup/80ml) muffin tray.

2 Line each of the muffin tray holes with 2 pieces of the bacon, overlapping to form a cup shape. Divide onion among bacon cups. Break one egg into small bowl then slide it into a bacon cup; repeat with remaining eggs.

3 Bake, uncovered, about 10 minutes or until eggs are just cooked and bacon is crisp around the edges. Carefully remove from the tray; serve with toast.

tip You can also use pancetta, a thinly-sliced Italian unsmoked bacon, in place of the bacon rashers in this recipe. Pancetta is also great used as a pizza topping.

scrambled eggs

preparation time 5 minutes cooking time 4 minutes serves 4

6 eggs
½ cup milk
2 tablespoons chopped fresh chives
30g butter
4 English muffins

using the microwave oven

1 Break the eggs into a medium bowl, add the milk and chives then whisk until mixed together. Put the butter in a shallow microwave-safe dish. Put the dish in the microwave oven, without a lid, and cook on HIGH (100%) for about 20 seconds or until the butter is melted. Using oven mitts, take the dish out of the microwave oven.

2 Pour the egg mixture into the dish.

3 Return the dish to the microwave oven and cook the egg mixture, without a lid, on HIGH (100%) for 1 minute. Take the dish out of the oven and stir the egg mixture with a wooden spoon. Repeat the cooking and stirring 2 more times so the eggs have been cooked for a total of 3 minutes. If the eggs are not set enough for you, then cook on HIGH (100%) for another 30 seconds.

While the eggs are cooking, split the muffins and toast them in a toaster or under a heated grill until lightly browned. Serve the eggs on the muffins.

tips It is important to use oven mitts when cooking in a microwave oven as some dishes can get hot.
★ We have served our scrambled eggs on English muffins but you can also use toast or bagels.

using the stove

1 Break the eggs into a medium bowl, add the milk and chives then whisk until mixed together.

2 Put the butter in a medium saucepan on the stove and turn the heat to medium. When the butter is melted, turn the heat to low.

3 Pour the egg mixture intothe pan and cook it, without stirring, until it begins to set around the edge. Using a wooden spoon, gently stir the egg mixture until it looks firm but is still a bit creamy.

tip Before you start eating, fill the pan or dish with cold water as this will make it easier to clean.

baked eggs with ham and cheese

preparation time 10 minutes cooking time 10 minutes serves 4

50g shaved ham, chopped coarsely
2 spring onions, chopped finely
4 eggs
⅓ cup (40g) coarsely grated cheddar cheese

1 Preheat oven to moderate (180°C/160°C fan-assisted). Grease four ½-cup (125ml) ovenproof dishes.

2 Divide ham and onion among dishes. Break one egg into small bowl, then carefully slide egg from bowl over ham and onion in dish. Repeat with remaining eggs. Sprinkle dishes with equal amounts of cheese.

3 Place dishes on oven tray; bake, uncovered, about 10 minutes or until egg yolk is just set.

Using a sharp knife, chop the ham coarsely on a chopping board.

Break eggs one at a time into a small bowl before sliding into baking dishes.

tip Break eggs, one at a time, into a small bowl before combining them. This way, if one is bad, you can throw it out without ruining the rest. And by sliding the egg into the baking dish you are less likely to splash or to break the yolk.

cheese omelette

preparation time 5 minutes
cooking time 5 minutes serves 1

2 eggs
1 tablespoon water
2 teaspoons butter
¼ cup grated cheddar cheese

1 Break the eggs into a small jug. Add the water then beat with a fork until mixed together. Put the butter in a medium frying pan on the stove and turn the heat to high. When the butter is melted, tilt the pan to cover the base and halfway up the side with the butter. Pour the egg mixture into the pan.

2 When the egg starts to set, tilt the pan and, using a wooden spoon, push the edge of the omelette from the side of the pan. This will let the uncooked egg run under the cooked egg so it will cook too.

3 Continue cooking the omelette until the egg mixture is nearly set. The top should still look creamy. Sprinkle the cheese over the top.

4 Hold the pan with one hand; with the other hand, use a spatula to fold the omelette in half. Still using the oven mitt to hold the pan, slide the omelette onto a serving plate.

tip Vary your omelette by adding herbs such as parsley to the raw egg mixture, or add some chopped ham to the cheese.

tips You can make the vegetable filling a little ahead of time but only make the omelettes just before you want to serve them.

★ We used sliced button mushrooms for our omelettes but you can choose any variety you like.

★ By breaking the eggs one at a time into a small bowl first, you will be able to discard any egg that's bad without ruining the others.

mushroom, pepper and cheese omelettes

preparation time 15 minutes **cooking time** 15 minutes **serves** 4

20g butter
1 small red pepper (150g), sliced thinly
200g mushrooms, sliced thinly
2 tablespoons finely chopped fresh chives
8 eggs
1 tablespoon milk
4 spring onions, sliced thinly
½ cup (60g) coarsely grated cheddar cheese

1 Melt butter in large frying pan; cook pepper, mushroom and chives, stirring occasionally, about 4 minutes or until vegetables soften. Drain vegetable filling on absorbent-paper-lined plate; cover with another plate or foil to keep warm.

2 One at a time, break eggs into small bowl, then pour into large jug. When all eggs are in jug, whisk until well combined and frothy, then whisk in milk and onion.

3 Pour half of the egg mixture into the frying pan you used for the vegetables; tilt pan to cover base with egg mixture. Cook over medium heat about 4 minutes or until omelette is just set. Carefully spoon half of the vegetable filling onto one half of the omelette; sprinkle half of the cheese over vegetable filling. Use a spatula to lift and fold the unfilled half over the vegetable filling. Carefully slide omelette onto plate; cover with foil to keep warm.

4 Make one more omelette with remaining egg mixture, vegetable filling and cheese. Cut each omelette in half; place one half on each serving plate.

vegetable frittata

preparation time 15 minutes   cooking time 1 hour   serves 6

2 medium potatoes (400g), peeled, cut into 1cm slices
1 medium sweet potato (400g), peeled, cut into 1cm slices
10 eggs
½ cup (125ml) cream
1 cup (80g) coarsely grated parmesan cheese
½ cup (60g) coarsely grated cheddar cheese
50g rocket leaves
2 tablespoons thinly sliced fresh basil

1 Preheat oven to moderate (180°C/160°C fan-assisted). Grease deep 19cm-square cake tin; line base and sides with baking parchment, bringing paper 5cm above edges.

2 Boil, steam or microwave potato and sweet potato, separately, until just tender; drain.

3 Meanwhile, break one egg into small bowl, then pour into large jug. Repeat with remaining eggs. When all eggs are in jug, whisk until well combined, then whisk in cream and both cheeses.

4 Layer potato slices in cake tin; top with rocket, then sweet potato slices, then basil. Carefully pour egg mixture over vegetables.

5 Bake frittata, covered, 45 minutes. Remove from oven; stand frittata in tin for 5 minutes before slicing into wedges.

tips Baby spinach leaves can be used instead of the rocket if you like, and you can substitute sliced cooked butternut squash for the sweet potato.
★ To make a frittata that is lower in fat, replace the cream with a semi-skimmed (2 per cent fat) milk.

did you know?

A frittata is the Italian version of a filled omelette, the main difference being that it is oven-baked, while an omelette is cooked on top of the stove.

Spread the rocket leaves over the potato.

Pour the egg mixture carefully over the vegetables so they stay in place.

Don't cut the frittata until it's been out of the oven for 5 minutes, to let it set.

breakfast on a muffin

You can use either four english muffins split into halves or, if you prefer, eight crumpets with any one of the following topping recipes.

tomato, spinach and cheese

preparation time 10 minutes
cooking time 5 minutes

Preheat grill. Layer 60g baby spinach leaves, two thinly sliced medium tomatoes and ⅔ cup (80g) grated cheddar cheese on muffins or crumpets. Place on baking tray under preheated grill until cheese bubbles and melts.

banana, peanut butter and honey

preparation time 5 minutes
cooking time 5 minutes

Preheat grill. Spread ⅓ cup (95g) peanut butter then ⅓ cup (120g) honey on muffins or crumpets; top with two thinly sliced medium bananas. Place on baking tray under preheated grill until honey starts to sizzle.

mixed berry

preparation time 5 minutes
cooking time 5 minutes

Combine ½ cup (160g) raspberry jam with 1½ cups (225g) thawed mixed frozen berries. Spoon onto muffins or crumpets; serve with 1 cup (280g) yogurt.

tuna and avocado

preparation time 10 minutes
cooking time 5 minutes

Preheat grill. Using back of fork, mash one medium avocado, one drained 95g can tuna in spring water and 1 tablespoon lemon juice in small bowl. Spread over muffins or crumpets; sprinkle with ⅔ cup (80g) grated cheddar cheese. Place on baking tray under preheated grill until cheese bubbles and melts.

Pour ¼ cup of the batter into the frying pan for each pancake.

Turn pancake with spatula to lightly brown other side.

buttermilk pancakes with raspberry butter

preparation time 10 minutes (plus refrigeration time)
cooking time 20 minutes makes 16

2 cups (300g) self-raising flour
⅓ cup (75g) caster sugar
2 eggs, beaten lightly
600ml buttermilk
50g unsalted butter, melted
1 tablespoon finely grated lemon rind
cooking-oil spray
125g unsalted butter, softened
¼ cup (80g) raspberry jam

1 Sift flour and sugar into large bowl; whisk eggs, buttermilk, melted butter and rind in medium bowl. Gradually whisk egg mixture into flour mixture; whisk until mixture makes a smooth batter. Transfer batter to large jug. Cover; refrigerate batter 30 minutes.

2 Lightly spray large heavy-base frying pan with cooking-oil spray. Pour ¼ cup batter into heated pan for each pancake; you can cook four at a time. Cook pancakes, uncovered, until bubbles appear on surface; turn each pancake with spatula to lightly brown other side. Cover pancakes on plate with foil; make 12 more pancakes with remaining batter.

3 Beat softened butter in small bowl with electric mixer until light and creamy. Add jam; continue beating until combined.

4 Serve pancakes topped with raspberry butter.

did you know?

Buttermilk, contrary to its name, doesn't contain any butter, but it is found alongside other types of fresh milk in the supermarket dairy section. It is the liquid left after the cream is separated from milk, and is very low in fat. As well as making pancakes and scones with it, you can use buttermilk in homemade salad dressings and soups.

hassle-free hotcakes

preparation time 10 minutes (plus resting time) cooking time 40 minutes
makes 10

1¾ cups self-raising flour
¼ teaspoon bicarbonate of soda
2 eggs
1¼ cups milk
⅓ cup caster sugar
30g soft butter

1 Sift the flour and bicarbonate of soda into a large bowl.

2 Make a hole in the centre of the flour with your fingers.

3 Break the eggs into a large jug. Add the milk and sugar and beat with a fork until mixed together.

tip Start preparing the hotcakes about 1 hour before you're ready to eat them. The batter has to rest in the refrigerator for ½ hour before you start cooking.

4 Put the bowl of flour on a damp folded tea towel to stop the bowl moving. Gradually whisk the milk mixture into the flour and keep whisking until it is smooth. Cover the bowl with cling film and put it in the refrigerator for 30 minutes.

5 Put about ½ teaspoon of the butter in a medium frying pan on the stove and turn the heat to medium. Fill a ¼ cup measure with the milk and flour mixture (batter). When the butter is melted, pour the batter into the pan.

6 Cook the hotcake for about 2 minutes or until it is just set around the edge and small bubbles have burst on the surface. Using a spatula, turn the hotcake over and cook it for another 2 minutes or until the other side is lightly browned. Take the hotcake out of the pan and place it on a serving plate (you can stack the hotcakes until you're ready to eat). Cook the rest of the batter in the same way using the rest of the butter.

topping them off

bananas with maple syrup
Top the hotcakes with sliced bananas then drizzle maple syrup over them.

lemon, butter and sugar
Put a dob of butter on each hotcake, pour some lemon juice over and sprinkle with sugar.

nutty berry treat
Spread the hotcakes with Nutella and scatter over a few sliced fresh strawberries.

waffles with maple syrup and strawberries

preparation time 15 minutes cooking time 10 minutes serves 4

8 packaged Belgian-style waffles (400g)
20g butter
500g strawberries, hulled, sliced thickly
½ cup (125ml) pure maple syrup

1 Preheat oven to moderately low (170°C/150°C fan-assisted).

2 Place waffles, in single layer, on baking tray; heat, in oven, about 8 minutes.

3 Meanwhile, melt butter in medium frying pan; cook strawberries, stirring gently, about 2 minutes or until just heated through. Add maple syrup; cook, stirring gently, until heated through.

4 Divide waffles among serving plates; top with the strawberry maple syrup mixture.

did you know?

Pure maple syrup is a rich-tasting, dark-brown syrup made from the sap of maple trees; the syrup that is called maple-flavoured (or pancake syrup) on the label isn't the 'real thing' and is not a good substitute.

Stir the strawberries gently so that they hold their shape and don't become mushy.

tips You can find Belgian-style waffles on supermarket shelves and in most most delicatessens.
★ Hulling a strawberry means cutting around the leafy part at the top to remove the green and a bit of the core.

You might want to make your lunch for school or to share with friends at the park: make some great sandwiches or try a smooth soup to fill your thermos. For weekends and holidays, practice your skills with pizza-making or chopping salads and creating your own dressings!

lunches and
lunch boxes

sensational sandwiches

hummus and cucumber

Spread one slice of bread with 1 tablespoon prepared hummus; top with ⅛ of a thinly sliced cucumber and another slice of bread.

tuna and sweetcorn

Combine half of a drained 185g can tuna in springwater, 2 tablespoons drained and rinsed canned sweetcorn kernels, and 1 tablespoon mayonnaise in small bowl. Spread mixture on one slice of bread. Top with ⅛ of a thinly sliced cucumber and another slice of bread.

fruit and nut

Spread one slice of bread with 3 teaspoons hazelnut chocolate spread; top with 1 tablespoon sultanas and half a thinly sliced small banana. Top with another slice of bread.

peanut butter and vegetables

Spread 1 tablespoon peanut butter over two slices of bread; top one slice with 1 tablespoon coarsely grated carrot and 1 tablespoon coarsely grated celery. Top with remaining bread slice.

egg, tomato and mayonnaise

Combine half a deseeded, finely chopped small tomato, 1 tablespoon coarsely grated cheddar cheese, one coarsely chopped hard-boiled egg, and 1 tablespoon mayonnaise in small bowl. Spread mixture on one slice of bread; top with ¼ cup loosely packed mixed lettuce leaves and another slice of bread.

cream cheese, chicken and avocado

Combine ¼ cup (40g) coarsely chopped barbecued chicken, ¼ of a coarsely chopped small avocado, and 1 teaspoon lemon juice in small bowl. Spread 1 tablespoon spreadable cream cheese on one slice of bread; top with chicken mixture, ¼ cup loosely packed mixed salad leaves, and another slice of bread.

cheese and vegetables

Combine 2 tablespoons coarsely grated cheddar cheese, 2 tablespoons coarsely grated carrot, 2 tablespoons coarsely grated celery, and 1 tablespoon soured cream in small bowl. Spread mixture over one slice of bread; top with another slice of bread.

cheese, sausage and pickle

Spread 1 tablespoon of sweet mustard pickle over two slices of bread; top one slice of bread with one slice of cheddar cheese and one cold cooked thickly sliced beef sausage. Top with remaining slice of bread.

toasts and melts

cinnamon toast

makes 2

Spread ½ teaspoon butter on each of two slices of white bread. Combine 2 teaspoons caster sugar and 1 teaspoon cinnamon in small bowl; sprinkle over each slice of buttered bread. Toast under preheated grill about 2 minutes or until browned lightly.

ham, cheese and tomato melt

makes 2

Spread 2 teaspoons tomato chutney on each of two slices of white bread; top each slice of bread with half a slice of ham, a quarter of a thinly sliced tomato, and one slice of swiss cheese. Place under preheated grill about 5 minutes or until cheese melts.

turkey baguette melt

makes 2

Slice 10cm piece french bread stick in half horizontally; top each half with one slice of smoked turkey breast, a quarter of a thinly sliced green pepper, and one slice of edam cheese. Place under preheated grill about 5 minutes or until cheese melts.

tuna salad on focaccia melt

makes 1

Combine half of a drained 185g can tuna in brine, 2 tablespoons mayonnaise, half of a finely chopped small red onion, and 2 tablespoons finely chopped fresh flat-leaf parsley in small bowl. Cut a 300g garlic focaccia into quarters; spread tuna mixture over one quarter, top with one slice of tasty cheese. Place under preheated grill about 5 minutes or until cheese melts.

mexican bagels

preparation time 5 minutes
cooking time 5 minutes serves 2

1 bagel
1 tablespoon bottled salsa
½ small avocado (100g),
sliced thickly
2 slices cheddar cheese

1 Preheat grill.

2 Split bagel in half horizontally;
spread 2 teaspoons of salsa over
each half. Top each half with
avocado and one cheese slice.

3 Place under grill about 5 minutes
or until cheese melts.

did you know?

The avocado is a tropical
fruit that contains fat but no
cholesterol. Apart from the olive,
it is the only high-fat fruit, but
because it's monounsaturated
(the heart-healthy 'good' fat we
also get from olive oil) it may
actually help lower cholesterol.
Rich in antioxidants (substances
that protect the body against cell
damage), avocados are also a
good source of vitamins B6 and
E, dietary fibre, potassium and
essential fatty acids.

spiced beef and hummus wraps

preparation time 15 minutes cooking time 10 minutes serves 4

800g thick beef boneless sirloin steaks
2 tablespoons Middle-Eastern spice mix
4 wraps
½ cup (130g) hummus
1 baby cos lettuce (180g)
2 large plum tomatoes (180g), sliced thickly
¼ cup (70g) Greek-style plain yogurt

1 Trim excess fat from the steaks. Sprinkle beef with Middle-Eastern
spice mix.

2 Cook beef on heated, oiled grill pan (or barbecue or pan-fry) about
5 minutes on each side or until cooked as desired. Stand 5 minutes
then slice beef thinly.

3 To serve, spread wraps with hummus, top with lettuce, tomato, beef
and yogurt; wrap to enclose.

tip Middle-Eastern spice mix is available from Middle Eastern food stores and most supermarkets.

tips It's best if you don't assemble the pizzas until you are ready to cook them.
★ You can use cabanossi (spiced Polish sausages) instead of the pepperoni, if you prefer.

mini pizzas

Spread pitta breads with tomato paste.

Sprinkle toppings on pizza.

ham, sausage and pineapple

preparation time 10 minutes   cooking time 10 minutes   makes 4

4 pitta pocket breads
⅓ cup (90g) tomato paste
150g pepperoni, sliced thinly
100g ham, chopped finely
½ medium red pepper (100g), chopped finely
440g can pineapple pieces in natural juice, drained
1½ cups (180g) grated cheddar cheese

1 Preheat oven to hot (220°C/200°C fan-assisted).

2 Spread each pocket bread with 1 tablespoon of the tomato paste.

3 Place pocket breads onto baking trays; top with cabanossi, ham, pepper and pineapple. Sprinkle with cheese.

4 Cook, uncovered, about 12 minutes or until cheese melts and is browned lightly.

antipasto and mozzarella mini pizza

makes 1

Spread 1 tablespoon sun-dried tomato pesto over small pizza base; top with four drained marinated artichoke quarters, 30g drained bottled char-grilled pepper, and ¼ cup (25g) coarsely grated mozzarella cheese. Place under preheated grill about 5 minutes or until cheese melts.

pesto chicken pitta mini pizza

makes 1

Spread 2 tablespoons pesto over 1 pocket pitta bread; top with ¼ cup (40g) coarsely chopped barbecued chicken and ¼ cup (25g) coarsely grated pizza cheese. Place under preheated grill about 5 minutes or until cheese melts.

Use fingertips to rub butter into flour.

Starting from one of the long sides, roll the dough tightly.

Use a serrated knife to slice roll; place slices in pan as they're cut.

pizza scrolls

preparation time 20 minutes   cooking time 30 minutes   makes 12

2 cups (300g) self-raising flour
1 tablespoon caster sugar
30g butter
¾ cup (180ml) milk
¼ cup (70g) tomato paste
2 teaspoons Italian herb blend
100g sliced mild salami, cut into thin strips
1 medium green pepper (200g), cut into thin strips
2 cups (200g) coarsely grated pizza cheese

1 Preheat oven to moderate (180°C/160°C fan-assisted). Grease 19cm x 29cm shallow baking tin.

2 Place flour and sugar in medium bowl; use fingers to rub butter into flour mixture until it resembles coarse breadcrumbs. Stir in milk; mix to a soft, sticky dough. Knead dough lightly on floured surface. Using rolling pin, roll dough out to form 30cm x 40cm rectangle.

3 Using back of large spoon, spread tomato paste all over base, then sprinkle evenly with herb blend; top with salami, pepper then cheese.

4 Starting from one of the long sides, roll dough up tightly; trim edges. Using serrated knife, cut roll carefully into 12 even slices; place slices, cut-side up, in single layer, in tin. Bake scroll slices, uncovered, about 30 minutes or until browned lightly.

chicken noodle soup

preparation time 10 minutes cooking time 5 minutes serves 4

3 cups (750ml) chicken stock
1 litre (4 cups) water
3 chicken breast fillets (600g), cut into 1cm strips
310g can corn kernels, drained
2 teaspoons soy sauce
2 x 85g packets chicken-flavoured 2-minute noodles
1 tablespoon chopped fresh chives

1 Combine stock and the water in large saucepan, bring to a boil; add chicken, corn, sauce, the chicken-flavour sachet from the noodles and the noodles to the pan.

2 Bring soup back to a boil, turn the heat to medium and cook about 5 minutes or until chicken is cooked through.

3 Serve soup sprinkled with chives.

Cut chicken into 1cm strips.

tip You need one large barbecued chicken weighing about 900g for this recipe. Discard the skin and remove all of the meat from the bones; using a fork, shred the meat coarsely.

chicken and vegetable soup

preparation time 30 minutes   cooking time 20 minutes   serves 4

1 cup (250ml) water
1.25 litres (5 cups) chicken stock
2 trimmed celery stalks (200g), sliced thinly
2 medium carrots (240g), diced into 1cm pieces
1 large potato (300g), diced into 1cm pieces
150g mangetout, trimmed, chopped coarsely
3 spring onions, sliced thinly
310g can corn kernels, drained
3 cups (480g) coarsely shredded cooked chicken

1 Place the water and stock in large saucepan; bring to a boil. Add celery, carrot and potato; return to a boil. Reduce heat; simmer, covered, about 10 minutes or until vegetables are just tender.

2 Add mangetout, onion and corn to soup; cook, covered, 2 minutes. Add chicken; stir until heated through.

minestrone

preparation time 25 minutes   cooking time 15 minutes   serves 4

1 tablespoon olive oil
1 small brown onion (80g),
chopped finely
1 clove garlic, crushed
2 bacon rashers (140g), rind
removed, chopped finely
1 trimmed celery stalk (100g),
grated coarsely
2 medium carrots (240g), grated
coarsely
410g can crushed tomatoes
2 cups (500ml) beef stock
1 litre (4 cups) water
½ cup (65g) short pasta
2 medium courgettes (240g),
grated coarsely
300g can white beans, rinsed,
drained
½ cup thinly sliced fresh basil
leaves

1 Heat oil in large saucepan; cook onion, garlic, bacon and celery, stirring, about 5 minutes or until vegetables just soften.

2 Add carrot, undrained tomato, stock, the water and pasta; bring to a boil. Reduce heat; simmer, covered, about 5 minutes or until pasta is just tender. Add courgettes and beans; bring to a boil. Remove from heat; stir in basil.

tips Many varieties of ready-cooked white beans are available canned, among them cannellini, butter and haricot beans; any of these is suitable for this soup.
★ You can use any small pasta for this recipe, such as little shells, small macaroni or even risoni.

tip Make sure the fresh tomatoes you use in this soup are very ripe.

fresh tomato soup

preparation time 20 minutes   cooking time 35 minutes   serves 4

700g medium tomatoes, deseeded, chopped coarsely
1 large brown onion (200g), chopped coarsely
2 trimmed celery stalks (200g), chopped coarsely
1 garlic clove, crushed
1 litre (4 cups) chicken stock
400g can tomato puree

1 Place tomato, onion, celery, garlic and half of the stock in large saucepan; bring to a boil. Reduce heat; simmer, covered, about 15 minutes or until vegetables soften.

2 Cool soup mixture for 5 minutes before blending or processing, in batches, until smooth. Pour each batch of processed soup into large jug while processing the remainder. Return all of the soup mixture to same pan. Stir in remaining stock and tomato puree; bring to a boil. Reduce heat; simmer, uncovered, 10 minutes.

tips You can substitute butternut squash for the pumpkin in this recipe. ★ Ginger, when fresh is also known as green or root ginger. It is the thick gnarled root of a tropical plant.

pumpkin soup

preparation time 25 minutes cooking time 25 minutes serves 4

2½ cups (625ml) water
1kg piece pumpkin, deseeded, chopped coarsely
1 large brown onion (200g), chopped coarsely
2 medium tomatoes (300g), deseeded, chopped coarsely
4cm piece fresh ginger (20g), grated
1 cup (250ml) chicken stock
150ml can light evaporated milk

1 Place the water, pumpkin, onion, tomato, ginger and stock in large saucepan; bring to a boil. Reduce heat; simmer, covered, about 20 minutes or until pumpkin is tender.

2 Cool soup mixture for 5 minutes before blending or processing, in batches, until smooth. Pour each batch of processed soup into large jug while processing the remainder. Return all of the soup mixture to same pan. Stir in milk; stir over heat, without boiling, until soup is heated through.

tips You should make the salad just before you're ready to eat it, but the salad dressing can be made ahead of time. Keep it in a glass jar, with the lid on, in the refrigerator.
★ Salad spinners make it easy to wash and dry lettuce leaves properly.

mixed salad

preparation time 15 minutes **serves** 4

½ cucumber
250g cherry tomatoes
1 medium carrot
8 cos lettuce leaves
1 medium avocado

salad dressing
½ cup vegetable oil
½ cup lemon juice
1 teaspoon Dijon mustard
2 teaspoons sugar

1 Slice the cucumber and cut the tomatoes in half on a chopping board. Peel the carrot and cut it into thick sticks. Tear the lettuce into bite-sized pieces. Cut the avocado in half lengthways (cutting around the seed), then twist the halves to separate them from the seed. Scoop out the seed with a spoon and carefully peel the skin away from the avocado. Cut the avocado into slices. Place the lettuce, carrot, cucumber, tomatoes and avocado into a large salad bowl.

2 salad dressing Put all the ingredients in a glass jar. Screw the lid on tightly and shake well. Drizzle the dressing over the salad and toss it together with salad servers.

thai beef salad

preparation time 20 minutes
cooking time 10 minutes serves 4

500g beef rump steak
60g bean thread noodles
½ cucumber (130g), sliced thinly
100g cherry tomatoes, quartered
1 small red pepper (150g), sliced
thinly
3 spring onions, sliced thinly
⅓ cup firmly packed fresh coriander
leaves
⅓ cup firmly packed fresh mint
leaves

thai dressing
¼ cup (60ml) lemon juice
1 tablespoon fish sauce
1 tablespoon brown sugar
1 tablespoon groundnut oil

1 Cook beef in heated oiled large frying pan until browned both sides and cooked as desired. Cover; stand 10 minutes, then slice beef thinly.

2 Meanwhile, place noodles in large heatproof bowl, cover with boiling water, stand until just tender; drain into colander. Using kitchen scissors, cut noodles into random lengths.

3 Make thai dressing.

4 Return noodles to same cleaned bowl with remaining ingredients and dressing; toss gently to combine.

thai dressing Place ingredients in screw-top jar; shake well.

did you know?

Originally a specialty from the Italian region of Puglia, orecchiette means 'little ears', a shape this pasta resembles. If you can't find orecchiette, use any small pasta you like – try penne, farfalle or little shells.

mediterranean pasta salad

preparation time 15 minutes cooking time 10 minutes serves 4

250g orecchiette pasta
2 tablespoons drained sun-dried tomatoes, chopped coarsely
1 small red onion (100g), sliced thinly
1 small green pepper (150g), sliced thinly
½ cup coarsely chopped fresh flat-leaf parsley

sun-dried tomato dressing
1 tablespoon sun-dried tomato pesto
1 tablespoon white wine vinegar
2 tablespoons olive oil

1 Cook pasta in large saucepan of boiling water, uncovered, until just tender; drain. Rinse under cold water; drain.

2 Meanwhile, make sun-dried tomato dressing.

3 Place pasta in large bowl with remaining ingredients and dressing; toss gently to combine.

sun-dried tomato dressing Place ingredients in screw-top jar; shake well.

chicken caesar salad

preparation time 15 minutes cooking time 5 minutes serves 4

3 bacon rashers (210g), rind removed, chopped coarsely
4 hard-boiled eggs, quartered
2 cups (320g) coarsely shredded barbecued chicken
700g cos lettuce, sliced thickly
½ cup (125ml) prepared caesar salad dressing
40g piece parmesan cheese

1 Cook bacon in heated small non-stick frying pan until crisp; drain on absorbent paper.

2 Place bacon in large bowl with egg, chicken, lettuce and dressing; toss gently to combine. Using vegetable peeler, shave cheese onto salad.

potato and sweet potato salad with honey mustard dressing

preparation time 15 minutes   cooking time 15 minutes   serves 4

4 medium potatoes (800g), unpeeled, chopped coarsely
350g sweet potatoes, peeled, chopped coarsely
150g green beans, trimmed, sliced thickly
2 spring onions, sliced thickly

honey mustard dressing
²/₃ cup (200g) mayonnaise
1 tablespoon water
2 teaspoons honey
2 teaspoons wholegrain mustard

1 Boil, steam or microwave potato, sweet potato and beans, separately, until just tender; drain. Place potato and sweet potato in large bowl. Rinse beans under cold water; drain.

2 Meanwhile, make honey mustard dressing.

3 Place beans, onion and dressing in bowl with potato and sweet potato; toss gently to combine.

honey mustard dressing
Whisk all ingredients in small bowl until combined.

tip Turkish bread is also called pide by some bakers and in some supermarkets. If you can't get hold if it, use ciabatta bread instead.

caprese salad bruschetta

preparation time 15 minutes serves 4

1 long loaf Turkish bread
30g baby rocket leaves
250g cherry tomatoes, halved
100g mozzarella cheese, sliced thickly
2 tablespoons finely shredded fresh basil
1 tablespoon extra virgin olive oil

1 Halve bread; reserve one half for another use. Cut remaining half crossways into four even-width pieces. Split each piece horizontally; toast both sides.

2 Place two bread slices on each serving plate. Top each slice with equal amounts of rocket, tomato, cheese and basil; drizzle with oil.

creamy potato and crispy bacon salad

serves 6

1kg baby salad potatoes
2 bacon rashers
2 medium onions
1 tablespoon olive oil
⅓ cup chopped fresh parsley

dressing
½ cup bottled French dressing
½ cup soured cream
40g packet French onion soup mix

1 Cut the potatoes in half on a chopping board. Put a large saucepan on the stove, put the potatoes in the pan, and use a jug to pour in just enough water to cover the potatoes. Turn the heat to high, cover the pan with a lid, and bring the water to the boil. Simmer the potatoes for 7 minutes or until they are just soft when you pierce one with a fork. Stand a large strainer in the sink. Using oven mitts, take the pan to the sink and pour the potatoes into the strainer. Run some cold water over the potatoes and let the water drain away. Leave the potatoes to cool for ½ hour.

2 While the potatoes are boiling, use kitchen scissors to cut the rind from the bacon, then cut the bacon into small pieces. Chop the onions on a chopping board. Put a large frying pan on the stove, turn the heat to medium, and put the oil in the pan. Wait 30 seconds, then add the bacon and onion and stir until the onion is soft.

3 dressing Mix together the French dressing, soured cream and the dry French onion soup mix in a small bowl. Cover the bowl and let the mixture stand for 30 minutes to soften the soup mix. Put the potatoes, bacon mixture and parsley in a large bowl, spoon over the dressing and gently mix together. Transfer to a salad bowl to serve.

tips This salad is made with cold potatoes, so you will need to cook them about ½ hour before you are going to eat.

main courses

Now you can really get serious and make dinner for your family! Try some great-tasting oven chips, a stir fry or some dipping wedges … really good ideas that everybody will like are not hard to make – and our options here are healthy too!

spaghetti bolognese

preparation time 15 minutes cooking time 50 minutes serves 6

1 large onion
1 clove garlic
1 medium carrot
1 small courgette
1 tablespoon olive oil
500g minced beef
2 x 425g cans chopped tomatoes
⅓ cup tomato paste
1 tablespoon beef stock powder
1 cup water
500g spaghetti

1 Finely chop the onion on a chopping board, crush the garlic, and finely grate the carrot and courgette. Put a large saucepan on the stove, turn the heat to medium, and put the oil in the pan. Wait 30 seconds, add the onion and garlic then stir until the onion is soft. Add the mince then stir with a wooden spoon until the meat is browned all over.

2 Add the tomatoes with their juice, the tomato paste, stock powder, water, carrot and courgette to the pan.

3 Stir the bolognese sauce with a wooden spoon to mix together. Turn the heat to low, simmer the sauce without the lid for about 30 minutes or until it thickens slightly, stir occasionally with a wooden spoon.

4 While the sauce is cooking, put another large saucepan on the stove. Use a jug to pour in onough water to come ¾ of the way up the side of the pan. Turn the heat to high, cover the pan with a lid and bring the water to the boil. Using oven mitts, remove the lid and add the spaghetti to the boiling water. When the water boils again, stir the spaghetti with a wooden spoon.

5 Boil the spaghetti, without the lid, for about 10 minutes or until it is just soft. Test it by taking a few strands of the spaghetti from the pan with a fork, letting it cool slightly then tasting it.

6 Stand a large colander in the sink. Using oven mitts, take the pan of spaghetti to the sink and pour the spaghetti into the colander. Let the water drain away. Serve the bolognese sauce over the hot spaghetti.

4

5

6

tip If you make the bolognese sauce a day before you want to eat it, the flavour will be better. Cover the saucepan and reheat the sauce. Take the lid off and stir a few times. Cook the spaghetti just before you're ready to eat.

vegetable lasagne

preparation time 25 minutes cooking time 50 minutes serves 6

400g butternut squash, peeled, chopped coarsely
500g swiss chard, trimmed, chopped coarsely
150g angel hair pasta
2 tablespoons olive oil
1 small leek (200g), sliced thinly
⅔ cup (160ml) vegetable stock
¾ cup (120g) ricotta cheese
¾ cup (180ml) cream
1½ cups (390g) bottled tomato pasta sauce
¾ cup (75g) coarsely grated pizza cheese

1 Preheat oven to moderate (180°C/160°C fan-assisted).

2 Boil, steam or microwave squash until just tender; boil, steam or microwave chard until slightly wilted. Drain vegetables separately. Mash squash in small bowl; reserve. Spread chard over sheets of absorbent paper, cover with more absorbent paper; reserve.

3 Meanwhile, cook pasta in medium saucepan of boiling water about 5 minutes or until just tender; drain. Rinse under cold water; drain.

4 Heat oil in medium saucepan; cook leek, stirring, about 5 minutes or until softened. Add squash and stock; cook, uncovered, stirring occasionally, about 5 minutes or until liquid is absorbed.

5 Meanwhile, combine chard in medium bowl with ricotta and cream.

6 Spread squash mixture over the bottom of 2-litre (8-cup) shallow baking dish; cover squash mixture with half of the pasta. Spread sauce over pasta; cover with remaining pasta.

7 Pour chard mixture over pasta, gently spreading to completely cover pasta. Sprinkle pizza cheese all over surface of lasagne.

8 Place lasagne on oven tray. Bake, uncovered, about 30 minutes or until lasagne is heated through and cheese is browned lightly.

Spread the wilted chard over sheets of absorbent paper to drain.

Mash the squash mixture until it is almost like mashed potato.

Cover pasta sauce with remaining pasta.

pizza

The basic pizza dough recipe makes two bases. Each of the topping recipes makes enough for one base. Each pizza serves four; the preparation time for a single pizza is around 45 minutes (plus standing time); the cooking time for each is 20 minutes.

basic pizza dough

2 teaspoons (7g) dried yeast
1 teaspoon sugar
½ teaspoon salt
¾ cup (180ml) warm water
2½ cups (375g) plain flour
2 tablespoons olive oil

Using a rolling pin, flatten dough and roll out to a 32cm round.

Carefully lift each pizza base onto oiled pizza pan or oven tray.

Use back of a large spoon to spread sauce over pizza base.

1 Combine yeast, sugar, salt and the warm water in small bowl, cover; stand in warm place about 20 minutes or until mixture is frothy.

2 Combine flour and oil in large bowl; stir in yeast mixture, mix to a soft dough. Knead dough on floured surface about 5 minutes or until smooth and elastic. Place dough in large oiled bowl, cover; stand in warm place about 1 hour or until dough doubles in size.

3 Meanwhile, preheat oven to very hot. Turn dough onto floured surface; knead until smooth. Divide dough in half; using rolling pin, flatten dough and roll each half out to a 32cm round.

4 Carefully lift each round onto oiled pizza pan or oven tray; cover each with one of the toppings shown here. Bake, uncovered, in very hot oven 20 minutes.

supreme

Using pastry brush, brush 1 teaspoon olive oil over pizza base. Place 2 tablespoons bottled tomato pasta sauce on base, using back of large spoon to spread sauce all over base. Sprinkle ½ cup (50g) coarsely grated pizza cheese over sauce, then top with 10cm piece (40g) coarsely chopped cabanossi sausage, four slices (45g) coarsely chopped danish salami, ⅓ cup (65g) thinly sliced red pepper and ⅓ cup (30g) thinly sliced mushrooms. Sprinkle another ½ cup (50g) coarsely grated pizza cheese over pizza. (Pictured on page 78.)

tangy barbecued chicken

Using pastry brush, brush 1 teaspoon olive oil over pizza base. Combine 2 tablespoons bottled tomato pasta sauce and 2 tablespoons barbecue sauce in small bowl; using back of large spoon, spread combined sauces all over base. Sprinkle ½ cup (50g) coarsely grated pizza cheese over sauce, then top with 1 cup (160g) finely shredded barbecued chicken and ⅓ cup (30g) thinly sliced mushrooms. Sprinkle another ½ cup (50g) coarsely grated pizza cheese over pizza. (Pictured top right.)

ham and pineapple

Using pastry brush, brush 1 teaspoon olive oil over pizza base. Place 2 tablespoons bottled tomato pasta sauce on base, using back of large spoon to spread sauce all over base. Sprinkle ½ cup (50g) coarsely grated pizza cheese over sauce, then top with 70g coarsely chopped ham and ⅓ cup (70g) coarsely chopped drained canned pineapple pieces. Sprinkle another ½ cup (50g) coarsely grated pizza cheese over pizza. (Pictured middle right.)

vegetarian

Using pastry brush, brush 1 teaspoon olive oil over pizza base. Place 2 tablespoons bottled tomato pasta sauce on base, using back of large spoon to spread sauce all over base. Sprinkle ½ cup (50g) coarsely grated pizza cheese over sauce, then top with ⅔ cup (130g) coarsely chopped drained bottled char-grilled pepper, 1 tablespoon finely chopped pitted black olives and ½ cup (75g) coarsely chopped semi-dried tomatoes. Sprinkle another ½ cup (50g) coarsely grated pizza cheese over pizza. (Pictured bottom right.)

ham and rocket pizza

preparation time 8 minutes
cooking time 20 minutes serves 4

2 x 335g pizza bases
140g pizza tomato sauce
200g gruyere cheese, sliced thinly
200g thinly sliced ham
100g baby rocket leaves
2 teaspoons extra virgin olive oil

1 Preheat oven to hot (220°C/200°C fan-assisted).

2 Place pizza bases on oven tray, top with sauce, cheese and ham.

3 Bake, uncovered, about 20 minutes or until cheese has melted.

4 Serve pizzas topped with rocket and drizzled with oil.

tip Don't assemble or cook pizzas until just before serving to keep them from becoming soggy.

steak sandwich with guacamole

preparation time 15 minutes cooking time 15 minutes serves 4

2 tablespoons olive oil
2 medium brown onions (300g), sliced thinly
4 beef minute steaks (400g)
1 large avocado (320g)
2 medium tomatoes (300g), deseeded, chopped finely
1 tablespoon lime juice
1 tablespoon finely chopped fresh coriander
4 small ciabatta breads, split horizontally
8 lettuce leaves

1 Heat half of the oil in large frying pan; cook onion, stirring, about 5 minutes or until browned lightly. Remove from pan; cover with foil to keep warm.

2 Heat remaining oil in same pan; cook beef, two at a time, until browned both sides and cooked as desired. Remove from pan; cover with foil to keep warm.

3 To make guacamole, use fork to mash avocado in medium bowl; add tomato, juice and coriander, mix gently to combine.

4 Toast cut sides of bread. Place bottom halves of bread on serving plates; top with equal amounts of lettuce, then beef, onion, guacamole and remaining toasted bread tops.

Using back of fork, mash avocado in medium bowl before adding tomato, juice and coriander.

stir-fry beef with rice

preparation time 25 minutes **cooking time** 25 minutes **serves** 4 to 6

2½ cups water
1½ cups long-grain rice
2 medium onions
2 large carrots
2 cloves garlic
2 tablespoons vegetable oil
2 cups broccoli florets

3 teaspoons cornflour
½ cup water, extra
¼ cup honey
¼ cup soy sauce
½ teaspoon beef stock powder
1 teaspoon sesame oil
500g beef strips

1 Put a medium saucepan on the stove. Put the water then the rice in the pan. Turn the heat to high then, when the water is boiling, turn the heat to low. Put a tight-fitting lid on the pan then simmer for 12 minutes. Turn the stove off, leave the pan on the stove with the lid on. After 5 minutes, remove the lid and lightly stir the rice with a fork.

2 While the rice is cooking, cut the onions in half on a chopping board. Cut each half into wedges. Slice the carrots into thin rounds then, if you like, cut each carrot round in half. Crush the garlic.

3 Put a large wok on the stove, turn the heat to high and put half the vegetable oil in the wok. Wait 30 seconds then put the onion, carrot and garlic in the wok. Stir-fry the vegetables with a wooden spatula or a wooden spoon until the onions are soft.

4 Add the broccoli then stir-fry with a wooden spatula for 2 more minutes.

5

6

7

5 Using oven mitts, take the wok from the stove and place it on a wooden board. Spoon the vegetable mixture into a large bowl. Put the cornflour into a medium jug, stir in the extra water then stir in the honey, soy sauce, stock powder and sesame oil until mixed together.

6 Return the wok to the stove, turn the heat to high and add the rest of the vegetable oil. Wait 30 seconds then put half the beef strips into the wok and stir-fry with a wooden spatula until the beef is lightly browned all over. Take the beef out of the wok and put it on a plate. Stir-fry the rest of the beef in the same way. Return all the beef to the wok. Keep the heat on high.

7 Give the honey mixture a good stir then pour it over the beef in the wok and stir with a wooden spatula until the sauce boils and thickens slightly. Return the vegetable mixture to the wok and stir with a wooden spatula until everything is hot. Serve the beef and vegetables with the steamed rice.

egg-fried rice

3 teaspoons groundnut oil
2 eggs, beaten lightly
1 teaspoon sesame oil
4 bacon rashers (280g), chopped
coarsely
1 medium brown onion (150g),
chopped coarsely
2 trimmed celery stalks (200g),
sliced thickly
1 clove garlic, crushed
4cm piece fresh ginger (20g),
grated finely
3 cups cold cooked white
long-grain rice
100g shelled, cooked small prawns
425g can baby corn, drained, sliced
½ cup frozen peas (60g), thawed
4 spring onions, sliced thinly
1 tablespoon soy sauce

preparation time 25 minutes   cooking time 25 minutes   serves 4

1 Heat one teaspoon of the groundnut oil in hot wok; add half of the egg, swirl wok to make a thin omelette. Remove omelette from wok; roll omelette, cut into thin strips. Repeat using another teaspoon of the groundnut oil and remaining egg.

2 Heat remaining groundnut oil and the sesame oil in wok; stir-fry bacon about 3 minutes or until brown. Add onion, celery, garlic and ginger; stir-fry over high heat about 3 minutes or until vegetables are just tender.

3 Add rice, omelette and remaining ingredients to wok; stir-fry until well combined and heated through.

tips One cup of long-grain rice will make 3 cups of cooked rice. Cook it the day before you need it. This will prevent the grains from sticking together as you make the fried rice.
★ Boil 1 cup (200g) of rice, uncovered, in a large saucepan of water until the rice is just tender. Drain rice then spread it on a tray, cover with absorbent paper; refrigerate overnight.

Spread cooked rice on a tray in an even layer and refrigerate until cold.

Swirl egg carefully along side of wok to make omelette.

Give a final gentle toss to fried rice to combine.

tip You need to start this dish about 1 hour before you're ready to eat. Any thick white fish fillet (that is, one with no bones) will work well in this recipe.

fish 'n' chips

serves 4

4 medium potatoes
2 tablespoons olive oil
4 small fish fillets
2 tablespoons plain flour
1 egg
½ cup cornflake crumbs
cooking-oil spray

1 Before you turn on the oven, put 1 shelf in the lowest position and 1 shelf in the middle of the oven. Turn the oven to very hot (230°C). Peel the potatoes on a chopping board then, using a crinkle cutter, cut them into 1.5cm chips. Put the chips and the oil into a large baking dish and stir to mix together. Put the chips on the middle shelf in the oven and bake, uncovered, for 20 minutes. Rinse the chopping board. On the chopping board, cut the fish into strips about 4cm wide.

2 Put the flour, egg and cornflake crumbs in 3 separate shallow bowls. Toss 1 piece of fish in the flour then shake off the extra flour.

3 Using a fork, beat the egg until it all becomes the 1 colour. Dip the fish in the egg then let the extra egg run off. Toss the fish in the cornflake crumbs. Dip the rest of the fish pieces in the flour, egg and crumbs, 1 piece at a time.

4 Lightly spray an oven tray with cooking-oil spray. Put the fish on the tray and spray the fish with some more cooking-oil spray.

5 Using oven mitts, take the chips out of the oven and place the dish on a wooden board. Using a spatula, and being careful not to burn yourself, turn the chips. Put the chips back on the middle shelf of the oven for 30 minutes or until they are browned. When the chips have 10 minutes left to cook, put the fish on the lower shelf of the oven as well. Cook fish, uncovered, for 10 minutes or until it is cooked through. To see if the fish is cooked, gently break 1 piece open with a fork to see if it is a solid white colour inside. Serve the fish with the chips.

tip Serve the chicken with lime wedges, a bowl of sweet chilli sauce and a green salad dressed with lemon vinaigrette.

oven-baked chicken with spicy wedges

preparation time 20 minutes cooking time 40 minutes serves 4

1kg potatoes, washed
1 egg white, beaten lightly
¼ teaspoon cayenne pepper
½ teaspoon sweet paprika
4 chicken thigh fillets (440g)
⅓ cup (50g) plain flour
2 egg whites, beaten lightly, extra
½ cup (50g) packaged breadcrumbs
½ cup (80g) cornflake crumbs

1 Preheat oven to hot (220°C/200°C fan-assisted).

2 Cut unpeeled potatoes into wedges. Combine potato, egg white, cayenne pepper and paprika in large bowl; toss to coat potato all over in spice mixture. Place potato, in single layer, in shallow, lightly oiled baking dish. Bake, uncovered, about 40 minutes or until browned lightly.

3 Meanwhile, trim fat from chicken. Using meat mallet, gently pound chicken until 5mm thick. Toss chicken in flour; shake away excess.

4 Dip chicken in small bowl containing extra egg white then toss in separate small bowl containing combined crumbs. Place chicken, in single layer, on oiled oven tray. Bake, uncovered, about 20 minutes or until browned both sides and cooked through.

5 Serve chicken with spicy potato wedges.

Use a sharp knife to cut potatoes into wedges.

Pound chicken with meat mallet until 5mm thin.

Dip chicken into combined crumbs to cover chicken completely.

crunchy lamb cutlets with potato wedges

serves 4 to 6

4 medium potatoes, unpeeled
2 tablespoons olive oil
6 trimmed lamb cutlets
1 tablespoon plain flour
1 egg
1½ tablespoons seasoned stuffing mix
1½ tablespoons cornflake crumbs
vegetable oil, for shallow-frying

1 Turn the oven to moderately hot (200°C). Wash and scrub the potatoes well, and dry them with kitchen paper. Cut each potato in half on a chopping board. Cut each half into wedges.

2 Brush a baking dish with some of the olive oil. Put the potato wedges in the dish, and brush them with the rest of the oil. Put the dish in the oven and bake for 25 minutes. Using oven mitts, take the dish out of the oven and place it on a wooden board. Turn the wedges over withtongs. Put the wedges back in the oven and bake them for another 25 minutes or until they are lightly browned.

tip You need to start the wedges about 1 hour before you're ready to eat them but you can cook the cutlets while the wedges are in the oven.

3 While the wedges are cooking, use a meat mallet to lightly hit the meat of the cutlets until they are even in thickness. Place the flour and egg in 2 separate shallow bowls. Using a fork, beat the egg until it all becomes the 1 colour. Mix the stuffing mix and cornflake crumbs together in a third bowl.

4 Coat 1 cutlet in the flour, then shake off any extra flour.

5 Dip the cutlet in the egg, then let the extra egg run off.

6 Coat the cutlet in the crumb mixture, then put it on a plate. Repeat steps 4, 5 and 6 with the rest of the cutlets.

7 Put a large frying pan on the stove, turn the heat to high, and put the oil in the pan. Wait for 1 minute, then turn the heat to medium and put half the cutlets in the pan. Cook the cutlets for 3 minutes or until they are browned underneath. Using tongs, turn the cutlets over and cook them another 3 minutes or until the other side is browned too. Remove the cutlets from the pan and put them on kitchen paper on an oven tray. Cover them with foil to keep them warm while you cook the rest in the same way. Serve the cutlets and the potato wedges with some salad if you wish.

cheeseburgers

preparation time 15 minutes   cooking time 15 minutes   serves 4

tip Use the best-quality, low-fat minced beef you can find to make these burgers.

500g minced beef
1 medium brown onion (150g), grated coarsely
1 teaspoon dried mixed herbs
2 tablespoons barbecue sauce
½ cup (50g) packaged breadcrumbs
1 egg, beaten lightly
½ cup (60ml) olive oil
4 hamburger buns, cut in half
4 lettuce leaves
2 medium tomatoes (150g), sliced thinly
1 x 450g can sliced beetroot, drained
4 slices cheddar cheese
½ cup (60ml) tomato sauce

Shape beef mixture into four patties that are roughly the same size.

1 Combine beef, onion, herbs, barbecue sauce, breadcrumbs and egg in large bowl. Shape mixture into four patties.

2 Heat oil in large frying pan, add patties; cook over medium heat about 15 minutes or until browned both sides and cooked through. Remove patties from pan; drain on absorbent paper.

3 Preheat grill.

4 Toast buns, cut-side up, under grill. Layer bottom half of bun with lettuce, tomato, beetroot, patties, cheese and tomato sauce. Top with remaining bun.

Cook beef patties until they are browned and cooked through.

lamb burgers with potato crush and rosemary gravy

preparation time 20 minutes cooking time 35 minutes serves 4

500g minced lamb
1 large brown onion (200g), grated coarsely
1 clove garlic, crushed
1 egg, beaten lightly
½ cup (35g) stale breadcrumbs
1 tablespoon olive oil
500g new potatoes
20g butter
1 tablespoon plain flour
1 cup (250ml) beef stock
1 tablespoon chopped fresh rosemary leaves
250g cherry tomatoes

1 Using hands, combine lamb, onion, garlic, egg and breadcrumbs in medium bowl. Shape lamb mixture into eight patties.

2 Heat oil in large frying pan; cook rissoles both sides, about 15 minutes or until browned and cooked through. Drain on absorbent paper; cover with foil to keep warm. Reserve pan with rissole drippings.

3 Meanwhile, boil, steam or microwave potatoes until tender; drain. Crush potatoes in medium bowl by smashing them a few times with potato masher; stir in butter.

4 To make rosemary gravy, add flour to rissole pan; cook, stirring, until mixture browns and bubbles. Gradually stir in stock; stir until gravy boils and thickens. Strain gravy; stir in rosemary.

5 Meanwhile, cook tomatoes, stirring, in heated small frying pan about 2 minutes or until split and just softened.

6 Divide potato among serving plates, top with rissoles, rosemary gravy and tomatoes.

Roughly crush potatoes by smashing them briefly with a potato masher.

Cook burgers both sides until browned and cooked through.

Cook the flour in same pan until mixture bubbles and thickens.

peanut chicken skewers and garlic bread

peanut chicken skewers

makes 8

4 chicken thigh fillets
1 small onion
1 clove garlic
1 tablespoon vegetable oil
2 teaspoons ground cumin
¾ cup chicken stock
⅓ cup crunchy peanut butter
¼ cup water
1 tablespoon plum sauce
2 teaspoons bottled sweet chilli sauce
2 teaspoons soy sauce
cooking-oil spray

1 Soak 8 short bamboo skewers in a dish of water for 30 minutes. On a chopping board, cut the chicken into 3cm pieces. Thread the chicken onto the bamboo skewers. Wash the board well. Finely chop the onion and crush the garlic.

tip The bamboo skewers used in this recipe are soaked in water first so they will not burn. You can also use metal skewers – these don't need to be soaked but spraying them with a cooking-oil spray helps the chicken slide off easily.

2 Put a medium saucepan onthe stove, turn the heat to high, and put the oil in the pan. Wait 30 seconds, turn the heat to medium then add the onion, garlic and cumin. Stir with a wooden spoon until the onion is soft.

3 Add the stock, peanut butter, water and the sauces to the pan then whisk the mixture together. Simmer, without a lid, for about 2 minutes until the sauce thickens slightly.

4 Lightly spray a griddle pan with cooking-oil spray. Put the pan on the stove and turn the heat to high. Wait 2 minutes then put half the skewers on the pan and cook for 5 minutes or until browned on 1 side. Using tongs, turn the skewers over and cook for another 3 minutes or until the other side is browned and and the chicken is cooked through. Put the cooked skewers on an oven tray and cover them with foil to keep them warm. Cook the rest of the skewers in the same way.

garlic bread

serves 2 to 4

2 long bread rolls
2 cloves garlic
80g soft butter

1 Turn the oven to 200°C. Split the bread rolls open then cut each roll in half. Crush the garlic.

2 Put the garlic and butter in a small bowl then stir to mix together.

3 Spread the garlic butter on the inside of the rolls.

4 Wrap the rolls in a pieceof foil. Put the garlic bread in the oven and bake for 30 minutes. Using oven mitts, remove the garlic bread from the oven and carefully unwrap the foil (it will be very hot) to serve.

pork satay

preparation time 25 minutes   cooking time 20 minutes   serves 4

¾ cup (210g) smooth peanut butter
⅓ cup (80ml) coconut cream
¼ cup (60ml) sweet chilli sauce
⅓ cup (80ml) chicken stock
1 tablespoon lime juice
500g pork strips
2 cups (400g) white long-grain rice
3 cups (750ml) boiling water
¼ cup (35g) coarsely chopped,
roasted unsalted peanuts
⅓ cup coarsely chopped fresh
coriander

1 Preheat oven to moderate (180°C/160°C fan-assisted).

2 Combine peanut butter, coconut cream, chilli sauce, stock and juice in small bowl.

3 Thread pork strips onto eight skewers. Place skewers, in single layer, in large shallow baking dish; spoon peanut sauce over pork. Bake, uncovered, about 20 minutes or until pork is cooked through.

4 Meanwhile, place rice in medium saucepan with the boiling water, stir until water returns to a boil; cover with tightly fitting lid. Cook rice over low heat for 15 minutes without removing lid. Remove from heat; stand rice in pan, still covered, for 5 minutes.

5 Divide rice among serving dishes; top with satay sticks then peanut sauce from baking dish, sprinkle with peanuts and coriander.

Thread the pork strips onto eight skewers then place in baking dish.

Spoon the peanut sauce evenly over the pork skewers in dish.

finger-lickin' chicken wings

1kg chicken wings
2 tablespoons tomato sauce
2 tablespoons worcestershire sauce
2 tablespoons brown sugar
1 tablespoon American mustard

dipping sauce
1 tablespoon American mustard
2 tablespoons tomato sauce
1 tablespoon worcestershire sauce
2 tablespoons brown sugar

Combine sauce ingredients in small bowl; cook, covered, in microwave oven on HIGH (100%) for 1 minute.

preparation time 10 minutes (plus refrigeration time)
cooking time 30 minutes **serves** 4

1 Preheat oven to hot (220°C/200°C fan-assisted).

2 Cut wings into three pieces at joints; discard tips. Combine sauces, sugar and mustard in large bowl. Add chicken; toss chicken to coat in marinade. Cover; refrigerate 3 hours or overnight.

3 Place chicken, in single layer, on oiled wire rack set inside large shallow baking dish; brush remaining marinade over chicken.

4 Roast, uncovered, about 30 minutes or until chicken is well browned and cooked through. Serve chicken wings with dipping sauce.

honeyed chicken drumsticks

serves 4 to 6

2 cloves garlic
5cm piece fresh ginger
⅓ cup soy sauce
⅓ cup honey
2 tablespoons water
1 teaspoon sesame oil
12 chicken drumsticks

1 Turn the oven to moderate (180°C). Crush the garlic. Put the ginger on a chopping board and carefully cut off the skin.

2 Pierce the ginger with a fork and grate it on the medium side of a grater. Brush the inside of the grater with a pastry brush to help remove the ginger.

3 In a large shallow ovenproof dish, mix together the garlic, ginger, soy, honey, water and sesame oil with a wooden spoon.

4 Put the drumsticks in the dish and, using tongs, turn them over to coat with the sauce mixture. Put the dish in the oven and bake, uncovered, for 40 minutes or until the drumsticks are cooked through.

tips You need to start the honeyed drumsticks about 1 hour before you want to eat them. ★ These drumsticks are yummy served cold with a salad and potato crisps for a great picnic lunch.

marinated pork ribs

preparation time 5 minutes (plus refrigeration time) cooking time 40 minutes
serves 4

4 slabs (1.2kg) American-style pork ribs
⅓ cup (80ml) plum sauce
2 tablespoons barbecue sauce
2 tablespoons tomato sauce
1 tablespoon soy sauce

tip A slab of American-style pork spareribs will consist of between 7 and 10 ribs each. After the meat is cooked, separate the ribs with a knife then eat them in your hands.

1 Place pork in large shallow glass dish, pour over combined sauces; turn pork to coat in marinade. Cover, refrigerate 3 hours or overnight.

2 Preheat oven to moderately hot (200°C/180°C fan-assisted).

3 Remove pork from marinade; reserve marinade. Place pork, in a single layer, on wire rack over baking dish (you might need two dishes).

4 Cook pork, uncovered, 20 minutes. Brush pork with reserved marinade; cook further 20 minutes or until cooked through.

Pour combined sauces over slabs of pork in large shallow glass dish; turn pork slabs to coat in marinade.

tip Place the minced beef mixture, taco shells, lettuce, cheese, tomato and salsa in separate bowls on the table, and let everyone assemble their own tacos.

beef tacos

preparation time 15 minutes cooking time 25 minutes makes 12

2 teaspoons olive oil
500g minced beef
1 clove garlic, crushed
1½ cups (375ml) water
2 tablespoons tomato paste
35g packet taco seasoning
12 taco shells
8 lettuce leaves, shredded finely
2 medium tomatoes (300g),
chopped finely
1 cup (120g) grated cheddar cheese
½ cup bottled mild chunky salsa

Preheat oven to moderate (180°C/160°C fan-assisted).

Heat oil in large frying pan, add beef and garlic; cook, stirring, about 5 minutes or until the beef is browned all over. Add the water, tomato paste and taco seasoning to beef mixture; stir until well combined. Bring to a boil; reduce heat, simmer, uncovered, about 10 minutes or until most of the liquid is evaporated.

Meanwhile, place taco shells, upside down, on oven tray. Heat shells in oven, uncovered, about 5 minutes or until heated through. Using oven mitts, remove tray from oven, place on a wooden board.

Divide beef mixture among taco shells; top with lettuce, tomato and cheese, drizzle with salsa.

veggie nachos

preparation time 15 minutes   cooking time 35 minutes   serves 4

1 tablespoon olive oil
1 medium brown onion (150g),
chopped finely
1 clove garlic, crushed
400g can chopped tomatoes
420g can red kidney beans,
drained, rinsed
230g packet corn chips
1 cup (120g) grated cheddar cheese
½ cup (120g) soured cream
1 tablespoon chopped fresh
coriander

1 Preheat oven to moderately hot (200°C/180°C fan-assisted).

2 Heat oil in medium frying pan; cook onion and garlic, stirring, about 5 minutes or until onion softens. Stir in undrained tomatoes and beans.

3 Bring mixture to a boil; reduce heat, simmer, uncovered, 15 minutes, stirring constantly, until mixture thickens slightly.

4 Place corn chips onto large ovenproof plate; pour bean mixture over chips, then sprinkle with cheese. Bake, uncovered, about 10 minutes or until cheese is melted. Serve topped with soured cream and coriander.

tip Eat nachos as soon as they're ready or the corn chips will go soggy.

roast chicken dinner

serves 6

tip You need to start making this roast dinner about 2 hours before you're ready to eat. See the instructions on the following pages.

1 medium onion
1 tablespoon butter
1½ cups fresh white breadcrumbs
1 egg yolk
½ teaspoon dried mixed herbs
1.5kg chicken
1 medium onion, peeled, extra
¼ cup olive oil
4 medium potatoes
1 tablespoon plain flour
1½ cups water
1 teaspoon chicken stock powder

1 Before you turn on the oven, put 1 shelf in the lowest position and 1 shelf in the middle of the oven. Turn the oven to moderately hot (200°C). Finely chop the onion on a chopping board then wash the board. Put a medium frying pan on the stove and turn the heat to medium. Put the butter and onion in the pan and stir until the onion is soft. Let the onion mixture cool for 5 minutes. Put the breadcrumbs in a medium bowl then add the onion mixture, egg yolk and mixed herbs. Stir to mix together.

2 Rinse the chicken inside and out under cold water, then pat it dry with kitchen paper. Put the chicken on a chopping board, use your hands to push the stuffing mixture into the chicken. Wash the chopping board.

1

2

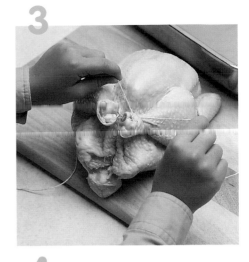

3   Tuck the tips of the wings under the chicken then tie the chicken legs
together with kitchen string.

4   Put the chicken and the whole extra onion in a flameproof baking dish.
Tuck the flap from the neck under the chicken. Brush the chicken with
1 tablespoon of the oil.

continued on page 108

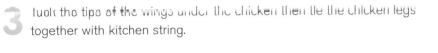

5 Peel the potatoes, wash them and pat them dry with kitchen paper. Cut the potatoes in half on a chopping board. Put the potatoes into another baking dish and brush with the rest of the oil. Put the potatoes on the lower shelf of the oven and the chicken on the shelf that is in the middle of the oven then bake for 30 minutes. Using oven mitts, take the potatoes out of the oven and put the dish on a wooden board. Leave the chicken in the oven. Close the oven door then turn the oven down to moderate (180°C). Turn the potatoes over with tongs and put them back into the oven for another 45 minutes.

6 Using oven mitts, carefully take the chicken out of the oven and put the dish on a wooden board. Move the potatoes to the shelf the chicken was on in the oven and bake for another 10 minutes. Using a skewer, pierce the chicken between the leg and thigh and look at the juices that run out. If the juices are clear the chicken is cooked, if they are pink, put the chicken back into the oven until they are clear when tested with the skewer. Using tongs, put the chicken and onion onto a large plate and cover with foil to keep warm.

7 While the potatoes finish cooking, make the gravy by putting the baking dish which had the chicken in it on top of the stove and turn the heat to medium. Add the flour and whisk until the mixture is bubbling.

8 Using oven mitts, take the baking dish from the stove and put it on a wooden board. Mix the water and stock powder together in a small jug and gradually whisk the stock mixture into the flour mixture. Using oven mitts, put the dish back on the heat and whisk the gravy until it boils and thickens slightly. Place a large jug in the sink then put a strainer on top. Being careful not to burn yourself, pour the gravy through the strainer into the jug. Remove the potatoes from the oven and serve with the chicken, onion and gravy. Don't forget the stuffing, which is delicious.

garlic and sage lamb racks

preparation time 10 minutes cooking time 25 minutes serves 4

3 large red onions (900g)
12 fresh sage leaves
⅓ cup (80ml) olive oil
2 tablespoons coarsely chopped
fresh sage
4 cloves garlic, chopped coarsely
4 x 4 French-trimmed lamb cutlet
racks (600g)

1 Preheat oven to hot (220°C/200°C fan-assisted).

2 Halve onions, slice into thin wedges; place in large baking dish with whole sage leaves and half of the oil.

3 Combine remaining oil in small bowl with chopped sage and garlic. Press sage mixture all over lamb; place on onion in dish.

4 Roast, uncovered, about 25 minutes or until lamb is browned all over and cooked as desired. Cover lamb racks; stand 10 minutes before serving.

parmesan mash

preparation time 5 minutes **cooking time** 10 minutes **serves** 4

4 medium potatoes (800g), peeled, chopped coarsely
30g butter
½ cup (125ml) milk
⅔ cup (50g) finely grated parmesan cheese

1 Boil, steam or microwave potato until soft; drain.

2 Mash potato in large bowl with remaining ingredients until smooth.

tip Potato mash can be made several hours ahead, covered and refrigerated. Reheat on LOW (10%) in a microwave oven just before serving.

roast butternut squash and potato with garlic

preparation time **15 minutes** cooking time **1 hour** serves **4**

750g butternut squash, chopped coarsely
750g medium potatoes, chopped coarsely
1 tablespoon olive oil
2 cloves garlic, sliced thinly
2 tablespoons fresh rosemary leaves
2 teaspoons sea salt

1 Preheat oven to hot (220°C/200°C fan-assisted).

2 Combine squash, potato, oil and garlic in large baking dish.

3 Roast, uncovered, about 1 hour or until vegetables are just tender and browned lightly.

4 Serve sprinkled with rosemary and salt.

roasted vegetables

roasted rosemary potatoes

preparation time 10 minutes
cooking time 50 minutes serves 4

1 bunch fresh rosemary
cooking-oil spray
1kg potatoes, unpeeled, quartered
2 tablespoons olive oil
3 cloves garlic, crushed

1 Preheat oven to hot.

2 Place rosemary in single layer to cover oven tray, spray with oil.

3 Combine remaining ingredients in large bowl, stirring to coat potato in oil.

4 Place potato on rosemary stems; roast, uncovered, in hot oven about 50 minutes or until potato is browned and tender, turning once midway through cooking time.

traditional roast potatoes

preparation time 15 minutes
(plus cooling time) cooking time
55 minutes serves 4

1kg potatoes, peeled, halved
2 tablespoons olive oil

1 Boil, steam or microwave potato until just tender, drain.

2 Preheat oven to hot.

3 When potato is cool enough to handle, gently scratch potato surface with a fork.

4 Place potato, cut-side down, on large oiled oven tray; brush potato all over with oil. Roast, uncovered, in hot oven about 50 minutes or until potato is browned and crisp.

tips Several potato varieties are well suited to roasting, including desiree, red and king edward.
★ You can 'roll' the potatoes in a plastic bag with the olive oil and garlic until they are coated, to avoid dirtying a bowl. Squeeze any remaining garlic and oil onto the potatoes before roasting.
★ There are many different baby vegetables suitable for roasting to be found at the greengrocer's. Look for baby beetroot, turnips, carrots and so on – they're beautifully sweet and flavoursome.

Placing potatoes on a bed of fresh rosemary

Scratching the surface of the potatoes with a fork

roasted baby vegetables

preparation time 15 minutes cooking time 40 minutes serves 4

500g baby onions
250g shallots
2 tablespoons olive oil
1kg tiny new potatoes, unpeeled
6 baby aubergines (360g), halved lengthways
250g cherry tomatoes

1 Trim off roots and remove cores of onions and shallots and discard.

2 Preheat oven to hot.

3 Heat oil in large flameproof baking dish; cook onions, shallots and potatoes, stirring, until vegetables are browned all over.

4 Roast vegetables, uncovered, in hot oven about 20 minutes, or until potatoes are almost tender. Add aubergine and tomatoes to baking dish; roast, uncovered, another 10 minutes or until aubergine is browned and tender.

Trimming roots from onions and shallots.

Adding aubergine and tomatoes to dish.

did you know?

Shallots (occasionally known as eschalots) are very mild small brown onions. Baby onions, also small and brown, are sometimes called pickling onions. Both varieties are excellent when slow-roasted, both with other small vegetables and on their own.

Tiny new potatoes are not a variety but an early harvest, having a thin pale skin that is easily rubbed off. New potatoes are good steamed as well as roasted, and can be eaten hot or cold in salads.

Create the perfect end to a
meal, or the best juicy, iced
snack: take some fresh
berries, full of goodness and
taste, mix them up a little
with all good things and the
hardest part – leaving them
to set!

ice-cream and desserts

chocolate sundaes

preparation time 5 minutes cooking time 5 minutes serves 6

2 litres vanilla ice-cream
½ cup (70g) crushed nuts
12 ice-cream wafers
100g marshmallows

hot chocolate sauce
200g dark eating chocolate, chopped coarsely
½ cup (125ml) whipping cream

1 Make hot chocolate sauce.

2 Place a little of the hot chocolate sauce in the bottom of six ¾-cup (180ml) serving glasses; top with ice-cream, more chocolate sauce, nuts, wafer biscuits and marshmallows.

hot chocolate sauce
Combine chocolate and cream in small saucepan; stir over low heat until chocolate is melted and sauce is smooth, do not overheat.

Stir chocolate sauce constantly over very low heat until just melted.

Top sundaes with equal parts pink and white marshmallows just before serving.

tip Make quick banana splits by cutting half a banana into wheels over the top of each sundae.

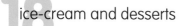

icy treats

frozen fruit and yogurt blocks

preparation time 5 minutes (plus freezing time) **makes** 6

Combine 1½ cups (420g) vanilla yogurt, 1 cup (150g) frozen mixed berries and 1 tablespoon honey in medium bowl; spoon into six ¼-cup (60ml) ice-block moulds. Press lids on firmly; freeze 6 hours or overnight.

tips For best results, the ice-blocks should be frozen for 6 hours or overnight.
★ To remove ice-blocks from moulds, dip into hot water for a few seconds, loosen lids and squeeze sides of mould. Ice-blocks should slide out easily.

lemonade ice-blocks

preparation time **5 minutes (plus freezing time)** makes **6**

Stir ¼ cup (60ml) lemon juice and ⅔ cup (110g) icing sugar in medium jug until sugar dissolves. Stir in 1 cup (250ml) sparkling mineral water. Pour mixture into six ¼-cup (60ml) ice-block moulds. Press lids on firmly; freeze 6 hours or overnight.

passionfruit and coconut ice-cream blocks

preparation time **5 minutes (plus freezing time)** makes **6**

Place 1 cup (250ml) softened vanilla ice-cream in small bowl; stir in ½ teaspoon coconut essence and 170g can passionfruit in syrup. Spoon mixture into six ¼-cup (60ml) ice-block moulds. Press lids on firmly; freeze 6 hours or overnight.

raspberry ice-blocks

preparation time **10 minutes (plus freezing time)** cooking time **5 minutes** makes **6**

Heat 1 cup (150g) frozen raspberries and ⅓ cup (55g) icing sugar in small saucepan over low heat, stirring occasionally, about 5 minutes or until raspberries soften. Using back of large spoon, push raspberry mixture through sieve into medium jug; discard seeds. Stir 1 cup (250ml) sparkling mineral water into jug. Pour mixture into six ¼-cup (60ml) ice-block moulds. Press lids on firmly; freeze 6 hours or overnight.

pineapple and mint ice-blocks

preparation time 5 minutes (plus freezing time) **makes** 6

Combine 1½ cups (375ml) pineapple juice, 2 tablespoons icing sugar and 2 teaspoons finely chopped fresh mint in medium jug. Pour mixture into six ¼-cup (60ml) ice-block moulds. Press lids on firmly; freeze 6 hours or overnight.

orange and mango ice-blocks

preparation time 5 minutes (plus freezing time) **makes** 6

Strain 425g can sliced mango in natural juice over small bowl; reserve juice. Blend or process mango slices, ¼ cup (60ml) of the reserved juice and ½ cup (125ml) orange juice until smooth. Pour mixture into six ¼-cup (60ml) ice-block moulds. Press lids on firmly; freeze 6 hours or overnight.

peppermint choc-chip ice-cream blocks

preparation time 5 minutes (plus freezing time) **makes** 6

Place 2 cups (500ml) softened vanilla ice-cream in small bowl; stir in ½ teaspoon peppermint essence, a drop of green food colouring and ¾ cup (75g) coarsely grated dark eating chocolate. Spoon mixture into six ¼-cup (60ml) ice-block moulds. Press lids on firmly; freeze 6 hours or overnight.

vanilla-caramel swirl ice-cream blocks

preparation time 5 minutes (plus freezing time) **makes** 6

Place 1½ cups (375ml) softened vanilla ice-cream in small bowl; spoon ice-cream
into six ¼-cup (60ml) ice-block moulds. Swirl 2 teaspoons caramel topping into
each mould. Press lids on firmly; freeze 6 hours or overnight.

layered banana split with caramel sauce

preparation time 10 minutes   cooking time 10 minutes   serves 4

⅔ cup (160ml) whipping cream
60g butter
¾ cup (165g) firmly packed brown sugar
1 cup (250ml) whipping cream, extra
500ml vanilla ice-cream
2 large bananas (460g), sliced thinly
½ cup (40g) almond flakes, toasted

tip Don't peel or cut the bananas until you're just ready to assemble this dessert because they'll turn brown quickly.

did you know?

Bananas are a good source of the minerals potassium, which helps our brains function properly, and phosphorous, essential for good health. They are also a great source of easy-to-digest fibre.

1 Stir cream, butter and sugar in small saucepan, over medium heat, until smooth. Reduce heat; simmer, uncovered, 2 minutes. Cool 10 minutes.

2 Meanwhile, beat extra cream in small bowl with electric mixer until soft peaks form.

3 Divide half of the sauce among four serving dishes; top with ice-cream, cream, banana, remaining sauce and nuts.

marbled ice-cream heart cake

preparation time 15 minutes (plus freezing time) **serves** 12

4 litres neapolitan ice-cream
600ml whipping cream
¼ cup (40g) icing sugar
few drops pink food colouring
2 x 50g packets Smarties

When soft enough, spoon ice-cream into cake tin.

Press down on film until ice-cream squashes into tin and top is flat.

Spread ice-cream cake quickly with cream, then decorate.

1 Take ice-cream out of freezer. Stand about 10 minutes or until just soft enough to remove from container. Using a large metal spoon, spoon ice-cream into 25cm heart-shaped cake tin (it should be big enough to hold 11 cups of liquid).

2 Cover top of ice-cream with cling film. Press down on film until ice-cream squashes into tin and top is flat. Freeze ice-cream overnight.

3 Next day, using a tea towel (the tin will be very cold), take ice-cream out of freezer. Remove cling film then run a knife around inside edge of tin. Put about 3cm of warm water in the sink and hold the tin in the water while you count slowly to five. This will melt the ice-cream a little and help the tin come off easily. Invert ice-cream cake onto serving plate, cover ice-cream loosely with cling film and return to the freezer for 30 minutes.

4 Beat cream, icing sugar and a few drops of food colouring in small bowl of an electric mixer until thick.

5 Take ice-cream heart out of freezer and remove cling film. Quickly spread top and side of heart with pink cream. Sprinkle with Smarties (if the ice-cream begins to melt at any time while you are decorating, put it back in the freezer to set). Return the heart to the freezer until you are ready to serve it.

tip Combine the chopped Raspberry Ruffles and some softened vanilla ice-cream; re-freeze then serve scoops drizzled with chocolate sauce.

rocky road ice-cream

preparation time 5 minutes   serves 4

110g Raspberry Ruffles, chopped coarsely
50g coloured mini marshmallows
2 tablespoons crushed toasted peanuts
1 litre vanilla ice-cream
⅓ cup chocolate sauce

1   Combine Raspberry Ruffles, marshmallows and nuts in medium bowl.

2   Spoon ice-cream into four serving bowls; drizzle ice-cream with chocolate
    sauce then top with Raspberry Ruffle mixture.

orange butterscotch tondue

⅔ cup (150g) firmly packed
brown sugar
25g butter
⅔ cup (160ml) cream
1 teaspoon finely grated orange
rind
2 tablespoons orange juice
100g white eating chocolate,
chopped coarsely
1 large banana (230g), chopped
coarsely
250g strawberries, halved
2 small pears (360g), chopped
coarsely
2 medium mandarins (400g),
segmented
18 marshmallows

preparation time 20 minutes (plus standing time) **cooking time** 10 minutes
(plus cooling time) **serves** 6

1 Stir sugar, butter, cream, rind and juice in medium saucepan until sugar
dissolves. Bring to a boil; boil, uncovered, 3 minutes. Remove from heat;
cool 5 minutes.

2 Stir in chocolate until fondue mixture is smooth; stand 5 minutes.
Transfer to serving bowl.

3 Arrange fruit and marshmallows on serving platter; serve with fondue and
skewers for dipping.

chocolate mousse

serves 8

200g dark chocolate
600ml whipping cream
3 eggs
⅓ cup caster sugar
50g dark chocolate, extra
8 sponge finger biscuits

tip Chocolate mousse takes about 2 hours to set, so you need to start making it at least 3 hours before you plan to eat.

1 Break the chocolate into pieces and put it into a small heatproof bowl which will sit over a small saucepan without slipping. Put this pan on the stove. Using a kettle, pour in enough boiling water to half fill the pan then turn the heat to high. Bring the water to the boil then turn the heat to low so the water is simmering.

2 Carefully put the bowl of chocolate over the pan of simmering water. When the chocolate starts to melt, stir it gently until it is completely melted. Using oven mitts or a pot holder, carefully take the bowl from the pan and pour melted chocolate into a large bowl.

3 Put half the cream into the small bowl of an electric mixer and beat it on medium speed until it thickens. Turn the electric mixer off.

microwave tip

A quick and easy way to melt chocolate is in the microwave oven. Break the chocolate into pieces and put them into a medium microwave-safe bowl. Put the bowl in the microwave oven and cook on HIGH (100%) for 1 minute. Using oven mitts, take the bowl out of the microwave oven and stir the chocolate. Repeat the cooking and stirring 2 more times for another 30 seconds each time or until the chocolate is just melted.

4 Break the eggs into another small bowl of an electric mixer, add the sugar then beat on high speed for 3 minutes or until the mixture is very pale and thick. Turn the electric mixer off.

5 Use a large wire whisk to gently stir the cream into the melted chocolate then gently stir in half the egg mixture until the chocolate and egg mixtures are mixed together. Do the same thing with the rest of the egg mixture. Put 8 serving bowls on a tray (they should be big enough to hold about ¾ cup of liquid each). Spoon the mousse into the bowls and cover each with cling film. Put the tray in the refrigerator until the chocolate mousse is just firm and well chilled.

6 Using a vegetable peeler, peel the side of the extra chocolate into a small bowl. This will give you tiny curls of chocolate. Whip the other 300ml of cream then put a spoonful on top of each mousse. Sprinkle the chocolate curls over the top and put the biscuits in the side of the whipped cream.

white chocolate and honeycomb mousse

preparation time 10 minutes cooking time 5 minutes (plus cooling time)
serves 4

2 eggs, separated
250g white eating chocolate, chopped coarsely
1 tablespoon caster sugar
1 teaspoon gelatine
⅓ cup (80ml) milk
300ml whipping cream
2 x 50g chocolate-coated honeycomb bars, chopped coarsely

Make sure there is no trace of yolk when beating egg whites, otherwise the mixture won't form soft peaks.

1 Place egg yolks, chocolate, sugar, gelatine and milk in small heavy-based saucepan; stir continuously, over low heat, until mixture is smooth. Transfer mixture to large bowl; cool.

2 Beat egg whites, in small bowl, with electric mixer until soft peaks form.

3 Beat cream, in separate small bowl, with electric mixer until soft peaks form.

4 Fold cream and honeycomb into chocolate mixture, then fold in egg whites. Divide mixture among four 1-cup (250ml) serving glasses; refrigerate mousse, covered, for 4 hours before serving.

Fold the combined whipped cream and honeycomb into the white chocolate mixture.

tips Start making this recipe at least 5 hours before you want to eat it to ensure the mousse has plenty of time to become firm.
★ Care must be taken when heating the chocolate mixture: if the heat is too high, the chocolate will 'seize', that is, become clumpy, grainy and unusable.

jelly custard cups

preparation time 5 minutes (plus cooling and refrigeration time) serves 6

2 cups (500ml) boiling water
85g packet strawberry jelly crystals
600ml carton prepared custard
3 strawberries, halved

1 Pour the boiling water into a large heatproof jug. Sprinkle jelly crystals into jug, stir until crystals are dissolved and mixture is clear; cool.

2 Place six ¾-cup (180ml) serving glasses on a tray. Pour jelly evenly into glasses.

3 Pour custard slowly over the jelly. Leave the glasses on the tray, cover each with cling film; put the tray in the refrigerator for about 4 hours or until the jelly is set.

4 Just before serving, place a strawberry half on top of each jelly cup.

mango and raspberry jelly

preparation time 20 minutes (plus refrigeration time)   **serves** 8

425g can sliced mango
85g packet mango jelly crystals
2 cups (500ml) boiling water
150g raspberries
85g packet raspberry jelly crystals
1 cup (250ml) cold water
300ml whipping cream

1 Drain mango in sieve over small bowl; reserve liquid. Measure ¼ cup mango slices and reserve. Divide remaining mango slices among eight ¾ cup (180ml) glasses.

2 Combine mango jelly crystals with 1 cup of the boiling water in small bowl, stirring until jelly dissolves. Add enough cold water to reserved mango liquid to make 1 cup of liquid; stir into mango jelly. Divide evenly among glasses over mango, cover; refrigerate about 2 hours or until jelly sets.

3 Divide raspberries among glasses over set jelly. Combine raspberry jelly crystals and remaining cup of the boiling water in small bowl, stirring until jelly dissolves; stir in the cold water. Divide evenly among glasses over raspberries, cover; refrigerate about 2 hours or until jelly sets.

4 Beat cream in small bowl with electric mixer until soft peaks form. Spread cream equally among glasses; top with reserved mango slices.

tip If you want to use fresh mangoes, you can use one weighing about 600g for this recipe. Peel it over a small bowl to catch as much juice as possible, then cut off mango cheeks and slice the cheeks thinly. Squeeze as much juice as possible from around the seed into bowl with other juice; add enough cold water to make 1 cup cold liquid to add to the jelly (step 2).

berry trifle with mousse filling

preparation time 25 minutes (plus refrigeration time) serves 6

200g packaged sponge cake, chopped coarsely
85g packet strawberry jelly crystals
1 cup (250ml) boiling water
½ cup (125ml) cold water
500g packet frozen mixed berries
100g packet vanilla instant pudding mix
2¾ cups (680ml) cold milk
½ cup (125ml) whipping cream
2 teaspoons icing sugar

1 Line bottom of deep round 2-litre (8-cup) serving dish with the sponge to make the bottom of the trifle a flat surface.

2 Combine jelly crystals with the boiling water in large jug, stirring, until jelly dissolves; stir in the cold water. Measure ¾ cup of the frozen berries, cover; place in the refrigerator. Stir remaining berries into jelly mixture.

3 Carefully pour jelly mixture over top of sponge pieces without moving the sponge pieces. Cover; refrigerate about 2 hours or until jelly sets.

4 Sprinkle pudding mix over milk in large bowl; whisk until combined. Pour pudding mixture over set jelly; refrigerate, covered, about 30 minutes or until pudding mixture sets.

5 Beat cream and icing sugar in small bowl with electric mixer until soft peaks form. Using rubber spatula, spread cream over trifle; sprinkle with reserved drained berries.

Line the dish with sponge pieces to make the bottom of the trifle flat.

Carefully pour the jelly mixture onto the sponge pieces in the dish.

Using a spatula, spread the cream mixture over trifle.

everyday
baking

These are the greatest-tasting things to make and store in a tin – if you can resist them! For those that need icing or decorating, you will have to wait until they cool. Find a big flat container which is airtight and you can make these a day or so in advance.

butterfly cakes

preparation time 30 minutes   cooking time 20 minutes   makes 24

125g butter, softened
1 teaspoon vanilla extract
⅔ cup (150g) caster sugar
3 eggs
1½ cups (225g) self-raising flour
¼ cup (60ml) milk
⅓ cup (160g) strawberry jam
300ml whipping cream, whipped
4 strawberries, sliced thinly
1 tablespoon icing sugar

tips Use two paper cases in each bun tray hole for added stability for butterfly cakes.
★ Cakes are at their best made on the day of serving. Once filled with the cream, refrigerate the cakes if you're not going to eat them right away.

1 Preheat oven to moderate (180°C/160°C fan-assisted). Line two deep 12-hole bun trays with paper cases.

2 Combine butter, extract, caster sugar, eggs, flour and milk in small bowl of electric mixer; beat on low speed until ingredients are just combined. Increase speed to medium, beat about 3 minutes or until mixture is smooth and changed to a paler colour.

3 Drop slightly rounded tablespoons of mixture into paper cases. Bake, uncovered, about 20 minutes. Turn cakes, top-side up, onto wire racks to cool.

4 Using sharp pointed vegetable knife, cut circle from top of each cake; cut circle in half to make two 'wings'. Fill cavities with jam and whipped cream. Place wings in position on top of cakes; top with strawberry slices and dust with a little sifted icing sugar.

Spoon the mixture into paper cases.

Fill the cavities with jam and cream.

Cut small circles from tops of cakes.

Blend or process mixture with buttermilk.

buttermilk scones

preparation time 15 minutes   cooking time 15 minutes   makes 16

3 cups (450g) self-raising flour
1 teaspoon icing sugar
60g butter, chopped
1¾ cups (430ml) buttermilk
300ml whipping cream
¾ cup (240g) strawberry jam

1 Preheat oven to hot (220°C/200°C fan-assisted). Grease and flour 23cm-square shallow cake tin.

2 Combine flour, icing sugar and butter in food processor; process until mixture resembles breadcrumbs. Add buttermilk; process until just combined (mixture should be sticky). Turn dough onto floured surface, knead lightly until smooth. Press dough out into 3cm thickness. Using a 5.5cm round cutter, cut dough into 16 rounds. (You will need to gently re-roll the dough to get the 16 rounds.)

3 Place scones into pan; they will fit comfortably, just touching one another slightly. Bake, uncovered, about 20 minutes or until browned lightly.

4 Beat cream in small bowl with electric mixer until thickened.

5 Serve warm scones, cut in half, topped with jam and cream.

Knead dough lightly on floured surface until smooth.

Cut dough into 16 rounds. Place rounds, barely touching, in pan.

carrot banana scones with orange cream

preparation time 20 minutes   cooking time 20 minutes   makes 12

2 cups (300g) white self-raising flour
½ cup (80g) wholemeal self-raising flour
½ teaspoon ground cardamom
40g butter
⅓ cup (65g) firmly packed brown sugar
½ cup mashed banana
⅓ cup finely grated carrot
¼ cup (30g) finely chopped walnuts
¼ cup (40g) finely chopped raisins
¾ cup (180ml) milk, approximately

orange cream
50g packaged cream cheese, chopped
50g butter, chopped
½ teaspoon grated orange rind
½ cup (80g) icing sugar

1 Grease 23cm (9in) round sandwich cake tin. Sift flours and cardamom into large bowl, rub in butter. Add sugar, banana, carrot, nuts and raisins, stir in enough milk to mix to a soft, sticky dough.

2 Turn dough onto floured surface, knead until smooth. Press dough out to 2cm (¾in) thickness, cut into 5.5cm (2¼in) rounds, place into prepared tin.

3 Bake in very hot oven about 20 minutes. Serve with orange cream.

orange cream
Beat cheese, butter and rind in small bowl with electric mixer until as white as possible. Gradually beat in sifted icing sugar.

spicy fruit scones

preparation time 20 minutes (plus standing time)   cooking time 15 minutes
makes 16

1¼ cups (310ml) hot strong black tea, strained
¾ cup (135g) mixed dried fruit
3 cups (450g) self-raising flour
1 teaspoon ground cinnamon
1 teaspoon mixed spice
2 tablespoons caster sugar
20g butter
½ cup (125ml) soured cream, approximately

1 Grease 23cm (9in) square shallow baking tin. Combine tea and fruit in small heatproof bowl, cover, stand 20 minutes or until mixture has cooled.

2 Sift dry ingredients into large bowl, rub in butter. Stir in fruit mixture and enough soured cream to mix to a soft, sticky dough.

3 Turn dough onto floured surface, knead until smooth. Press dough out to 2cm (¾in) thickness, cut into 5.5cm (2¼in) rounds, place into prepared tin.

4 Bake in hot oven about 15 minutes.

golden honey muesli scones

preparation time 20 minutes   cooking time 15 minutes   makes 12

2 cups (300g) self-raising flour
1 teaspoon ground cinnamon
20g butter
½ cup (65g) toasted muesli
¼ cup (60ml) honey
¾ cup (180ml) milk, approximately
1 tablespoon demerara sugar

1 Grease 20cm round sandwich cake tin. Sift flour and cinnamon into medium bowl, rub in butter, stir in muesli. Add honey, stir in enough milk to mix to a soft, sticky dough.

2 Turn dough onto floured surface, knead until smooth. Press dough out to 2cm thickness, cut into 5.5cm rounds. Place rounds into prepared tin, brush with a little extra milk, sprinkle with sugar.

3 Bake in very hot oven about 15 minutes.

bacon and egg scones

preparation time 20 minutes cooking time 15 minutes makes 16

2 bacon rashers, finely chopped
2¼ cups (335g) self-raising flour
90g butter, chopped
2 hard-boiled eggs, finely chopped
¼ cup (20g) finely grated parmesan cheese
2 tablespoons chopped fresh chives
1 tablespoon wholegrain mustard
1 cup (250ml) milk, approximately
2 tablespoons finely grated parmesan cheese, extra

1 Grease 23cm round sandwich cake tin. Cook bacon in pan, stirring, until crisp; drain, cool.

2 Sift flour into medium bowl, rub in butter. Add bacon, eggs, cheese, chives and mustard, stir in enough milk to mix to a soft, sticky dough.

3 Turn dough onto floured surface, knead until smooth. Press dough out to 2cm thickness, cut into 5cm rounds. Place rounds into prepared tin, brush with a little extra milk, sprinkle with extra cheese.

4 Bake in very hot oven about 15 minutes.

strawberry and almond cakes

preparation time 10 minutes   cooking time 15 minutes   makes 12

2 egg whites
60g butter, melted
⅓ cup (40g) ground almonds
½ cup (80g) icing sugar
2 tablespoons plain flour
2 small strawberries, sliced thinly

1 Preheat oven to moderately hot (200°C/180°C fan-assisted). Grease 12-hole (1 tablespoon/20ml) mini muffin tray.

2 Place egg whites in small bowl, whisk lightly; add butter, ground almonds, sifted icing sugar and flour. Whisk until just combined. Divide mixture among tray holes. Top each with a strawberry slice.

3 Bake, uncovered, about 15 minutes. Turn, top-side up, onto wire rack to cool. Serve warm or at room temperature, dusted with extra sifted icing sugar, if desired.

Whisk egg whites lightly with a wire whisk.

Spoon mixture into prepared muffin tray.

Place a strawberry slice on top of each cake before baking.

mini carrot cakes

preparation time 30 minutes   cooking time 35 minutes   makes 6

½ cup (125ml) vegetable oil
3 eggs, beaten lightly
1½ cups (225g) self-raising flour
¾ cup (165g) caster sugar
½ teaspoon ground cinnamon
2 cups (440g) firmly packed coarsely grated carrot
¾ cup (160g) drained crushed pineapple

cream cheese frosting
50g butter, softened
½ cup (120g) cream cheese, softened
2½ cups (400g) icing sugar

mini carrots
6 dried apricot halves
1 x 18cm green jelly snake

Roll apricot around jelly snake, so snake protrudes from one end.

Make several thin cuts in the jelly snake to make the 'carrot top'.

Place 'carrots' on cakes, with seam-side down into frosting.

1 Preheat oven to moderate. Grease 6-hole large (¾-cup/180ml) muffin tray.

2 Mix oil, eggs, flour, sugar and cinnamon in large bowl with a wooden spoon until combined. Stir in carrot and pineapple.

3 Pour mixture into prepared tray holes. Bake in moderate oven about 35 minutes. Stand cakes 5 minutes, then turn onto wire rack; turn cakes top-side up to cool.

4 Meanwhile, make cream cheese frosting and mini carrots.

5 Spread cold cakes with cream cheese frosting; place carrots on cakes, seam-side down.

cream cheese frosting
Beat butter and cream cheese in small bowl with electric mixer until light and fluffy; gradually beat in icing sugar.

mini carrots
Place apricots in cup, cover with boiling water; stand 10 minutes. Drain apricots, dry with absorbent paper. Cut jelly snake into six 3cm lengths. Place one piece of snake at the top of one apricot half; roll apricot half around snake, allowing snake to protrude from one end. Make several thin cuts in snake for carrot top.

tips Muffins are quick and easy to make; it is important that the wet and the dry ingredients in step 4 are only stirred together until just combined because overmixing produces tough, heavy muffins.
★ You will need a piece of cheddar cheese about the same size as a 3cm cube.

cheese, sweetcorn and bacon muffins

preparation time 20 minutes (plus standing time) cooking time 25 minutes
makes 12

½ cup (85g) polenta
½ cup (125ml) milk
3 bacon rashers (210g), rind removed, chopped finely
4 spring onions, chopped finely
1½ cups (225g) self-raising flour
1 tablespoon caster sugar
310g can sweetcorn kernels, drained
125g can creamed sweetcorn
100g butter, melted
2 eggs, beaten lightly
50g piece cheddar cheese
¼ cup (30g) coarsely grated cheddar cheese

1 Preheat oven to moderately hot. Oil 12-hole (⅓ cup/80ml) muffin tray. Mix polenta and milk in small bowl, cover; stand 20 minutes.

2 Meanwhile, cook bacon, stirring, in heated small non-stick frying pan for 2 minutes. Add onion to pan; cook, stirring, for another 2 minutes. Remove pan from heat; cool bacon mixture about 5 minutes.

3 Sift flour and sugar into large bowl; stir in corn kernels, creamed corn and bacon mixture. Add melted butter, eggs and polenta mixture; mix muffin batter only until just combined.

4 Spoon 1 tablespoon of the batter into each hole of prepared muffin tray. Cut piece of cheese into 12 equal pieces; place one piece in the centre of each muffin tray hole. Divide remaining batter among muffin tray holes; sprinkle grated cheese over each. Bake, uncovered, in moderately hot oven about 20 minutes or until muffins are well risen. Turn muffins onto wire rack. Serve muffins warm.

Use a fork to mix the muffin batter only until just combined.

Place one piece of cheese in the centre of each muffin pan hole.

Once muffins are well risen, turn them onto a wire rack.

blueberry muffins

preparation time 10 minutes   cooking time 20 minutes   makes 6

2 cups self-raising flour
¾ cup firmly packed brown sugar
1 egg
1 cup fresh or frozen blueberries
¾ cup milk
½ cup vegetable oil
2 teaspoons icing sugar

1 Before you turn on the oven, move a shelf to the middle of the oven. Turn the oven to 200°C. Lightly grease a 6-hole large muffin tray (the holes should be big enough to hold about ¾ cup of the muffin mixture). Put the flour and sugar in a strainer and use a wooden spoon to sift them into a large bowl.

2 Break the egg into a small jug and using a fork, beat it until it becomes 1 colour. Add the beaten egg, blueberries, milk and oil to the flour mixture, then stir until just mixed together — do not overmix.

tip You can also make delicious chocolate honeycomb muffins by adding ½ cup white chocolate chips and 100g chopped chocolate-coated honeycomb instead of the blueberries.

3 Spoon the mixture evenly into the holes of the prepared muffin tray. Put the tray in the oven and bake the muffins for 25 minutes. Using oven mitts, take the tray out of the oven and put it on a wire cake rack. Test the muffins with a skewer.

4 As soon as the muffins are cooked, carefully tip them out of the tray onto the wire cake rack. Just before you serve the muffins, sift the icing sugar over the top.

choc brownie muffins

preparation time 10 minutes   cooking time 20 minutes   makes 12

2 cups (300g) self-raising flour
⅓ cup (35g) cocoa powder
⅓ cup (75g) caster sugar
60g butter, melted
½ cup (95g) chocolate chips
½ cup (75g) chopped pistachios
½ cup (125ml) Nutella
1 egg, lightly beaten
¾ cup (180ml) milk
½ cup (125ml) soured cream

1 Grease 12 hole (⅓ cup/80ml capacity) muffin tray.

2 Sift dry ingredients into large bowl, stir in remaining ingredients.

3 Spoon mixture into prepared tray. Bake in moderately hot oven about 20 minutes.

raspberry and coconut muffins

preparation time 10 minutes cooking time 20 minutes makes 12

2½ cups (375g) self-raising flour
90g butter, chopped
1 cup (220g) caster sugar
1¼ cups (310ml) buttermilk
1 egg, beaten lightly
⅓ cup (25g) desiccated coconut
150g fresh or frozen raspberries
2 tablespoons shredded coconut

tips It is important not to overmix muffin mixture; it should be slightly lumpy.
★ If you are using frozen berries, use them unthawed; this will minimise 'bleeding' of the colour into the mixture.

1 Preheat oven to moderately hot (200°C/180°C fan-assisted). Grease 12-hole (⅓-cup/80ml) muffin tray.

2 Place flour in large bowl; using fingertips, rub in butter. Add sugar, buttermilk, egg, desiccated coconut and raspberries; using fork, mix until just combined.

3 Divide mixture among tray holes; sprinkle with shredded coconut.

4 Bake, uncovered, about 20 minutes. Stand muffins 5 minutes before turning, top-side up, onto wire rack to cool.

Rub butter into flour with fingertips.

Mix muffin mixture until just combined.

Sprinkle coconut on muffin mix.

quick-mix cupcakes

preparation time 20 minutes cooking time 20 minutes makes 24

125g butter, softened
½ teaspoon vanilla extract
¾ cup (165g) caster sugar
3 eggs
2 cups (300g) self-raising flour
¼ cup (60ml) milk

glacé icing
2 cups (320g) icing sugar
20g butter, melted
2 tablespoons hot water,
approximately

1 Preheat oven to moderate (180°C/160°C fan-assisted). Line two 12-hole bun trays with paper cake cases.

2 Combine ingredients in medium bowl; beat with electric mixer on low speed until ingredients are just combined. Increase speed to medium; beat about 3 minutes or until mixture is smooth and paler in colour.

3 Drop rounded tablespoons of mixture into each case; bake about 20 minutes. Stand cakes 5 minutes; turn, top-sides up, onto wire racks to cool.

4 Top cakes with icing of your choice.

glacé icing
Place sifted icing sugar in small bowl; stir in butter and enough of the hot water to make a firm paste; stir over small saucepan of simmering water until spreadable.
For chocolate icing: stir in 1 teaspoon sifted cocoa powder.
For coffee icing: dissolve 1 teaspoon instant coffee granules in the hot water.
For passionfruiticing: stir in 1 tablespoon passionfruit pulp.

variations

chocolate and orange
Stir in 1 teaspoon finely grated orange rind and ½ cup (95g) dark chocolate chips at the end of step 2.

passionfruit and lime
Stir in 1 teaspoon finely grated lime rind and ¼ cup (60ml) passionfruit pulp at the end of step 2.

banana and white chocolate chip
Stir in ½ cup overripe mashed banana and ½ cup (95g) white chocolate chips at the end of step 2.

mocha
Blend 1 tablespoon sifted cocoa powder with 1 tablespoon strong black coffee; stir in at the end of step 2.

Grease then line 20cm x 30cm baking tin with baking parchment.

Use fingers to press slice mixture over the base of prepared tin.

Using fingers, gently press the muesli topping onto the base.

apricot muesli slice

preparation time 25 minutes cooking time 30 minutes makes 20

100g butter
½ cup (110g) caster sugar
1 egg yolk
⅔ cup (100g) plain flour
¼ cup (35g) self-raising flour
1 tablespoon custard powder
½ cup (160g) apricot jam, warmed

muesli topping
¼ cup (90g) honey
50g butter
1½ cups (135g) rolled oats
1 cup (40g) cornflakes
½ cup (35g) shredded coconut
½ cup (75g) finely chopped dried apricots

1 Preheat oven to moderate. Grease then line 20cm x 30cm baking tin with baking parchment.

2 Beat butter, sugar and egg yolk in small bowl with electric mixer until light and fluffy. Stir in sifted combined flours and custard powder. Using fingers, press mixture over base of prepared tin. Bake, uncovered, in moderate oven about 15 minutes or until browned lightly.

3 Meanwhile, make muesli topping.

4 Remove slice from oven, spread with jam. Sprinkle muesli topping over jam, pressing gently with fingers. Return to oven; bake another 15 minutes. Cool slice in tin; cut into 5cm x 6cm pieces to serve.

muesli topping
Heat honey and butter in small saucepan until butter melts; transfer to large bowl. Stir in remaining ingredients.

tips You can make the slice different if you want to—try adding ¾ cup dark chocolate chips, or ¾ cup sultanas, or ¾ cup chopped dried apricots in with the oats (see Step 1).
★ This recipe is a great lunch-box treat. It will keep in an airtight container for up to four days, so you can make it on the weekend to take to school.

oat slice

preparation time 20 minutes   cooking time 35 minutes (plus standing time)
makes 30

1 cup (90g) rolled oats
1 cup (150g) plain flour
1 cup (220g) firmly packed brown sugar
½ cup (40g) desiccated coconut
125g butter, chopped coarsely
2 tablespoons golden syrup
1 tablespoon water
½ teaspoon bicarbonate of soda

1 Turn the oven to 160°C. Grease a 26cm x 32cm Swiss roll tin and cover the base with baking parchment. Put the oats, flour, sugar and coconut in a large bowl and stir to mix together.

2 Chop the butter. Put a medium saucepan on the stove and turn the heat to medium. Put the butter, golden syrup and water in the pan and stir the mixture with a wooden spoon until the butter is melted.

3 Take the pan off the stove and put it on a wooden board. Add the bicarbonate of soda to the butter mixture (it will froth and bubble).

4 Pour this butter mixture into the oat mixture and stir with a wooden spoon until all the ingredients are mixed together.

5 Sprinkle the mixture evenly into the prepared tin, then press down on the slice with your hands until it is flat. Put the tin in the oven and bake the slice for 35 minutes (it should feel firm when you touch it). Using oven mitts, take the pan out of the oven and place it on a wooden board. Leave the slice in the tin to cool for about 15 minutes. Turn the slice over onto the wooden board and remove the tin then the baking parchment. Cut the slice into pieces about 5cm square.

beetroot cake

preparation time 25 minutes cooking time 1 hour 30 minutes serves 22

3 small fresh beetroot (250g), trimmed
250g butter, softened
3 teaspoons finely grated lemon rind
1 cup (220g) caster sugar
4 eggs
1 cup (150g) currants
1 cup (150g) plain flour
1 cup (150g) self-raising flour

1 Position oven shelves; preheat oven to moderate. Grease deep 20cm-round cake tin; line base and sides with baking parchment.

2 Using a vegetable peeler, peel beetroot thinly; coarsely grate beetroot.

3 Beat butter, rind and sugar in small bowl with electric mixer until light and fluffy. Beat in eggs, one at a time, beating until just combined between additions. Mixture might curdle at this stage, but will come together later.

4 Transfer butter mixture to large bowl. Using wooden spoon, stir in beetroot, currants and flours. Spread mixture into prepared tin.

5 Bake cake in moderate oven about 1½ hours.

6 Stand cake 10 minutes, then turn onto wire rack; turn top-side up to cool. Dust with sifted icing sugar, if desired.

Peeling beetroot with vegetable peeler

Coarsely grating beetroot

tips It's a good idea to wear disposable gloves when peeling and grating beetroot, as it will stain your skin. If you're using a wooden chopping board, wash it as fast as possible after beetroot has come into contact with it to remove stains. Scrubbing the board with coarse cooking salt should help remove any stubborn stains.

★ The same amount of coarsely grated carrot or courgette can be substituted for beetroot.

★ Sultanas, chopped raisins or finely chopped pitted dates can be substituted for currants.

Spreading mixture into prepared pan

family chocolate cake with fudge frosting

preparation time 20 minutes **cooking time** 1 hour (plus cooling and refrigeration time) **serves** 20

2 cups (500ml) water
3 cups (660g) caster sugar
250g butter, chopped
⅓ cup (35g) cocoa powder
1 teaspoon bicarbonate of soda
3 cups (450g) self-raising flour
4 eggs, beaten lightly

fudge frosting

90g butter
⅓ cup (80ml) water
½ cup (110g) caster sugar
1½ cups (240g) icing sugar
⅓ cup (35g) cocoa powder

fudge frosting
Combine butter, the water and caster sugar in small saucepan; stir over heat, without boiling, until sugar dissolves. Sift icing sugar and cocoa into small bowl then gradually stir in hot butter mixture. Cover; refrigerate about 20 minutes or until frosting thickens. Beat with wooden spoon until spreadable.

1 Preheat oven to moderate (180°C/160°C fan-assisted). Grease deep 26.5cm x 33cm (14-cup/3.5-litre) baking tin; line base with baking parchment.

2 Combine the water, sugar, butter and combined sifted cocoa and soda in medium saucepan; stir over heat, without boiling, until sugar dissolves. Bring to a boil; reduce heat; simmer, uncovered, 5 minutes. Transfer mixture to large bowl; cool to room temperature.

3 Add flour and egg to mixture; beat with electric mixer until mixture is smooth and changed to a paler colour. Pour mixture into tin.

4 Bake, uncovered, about 50 minutes. Stand cake 10 minutes before turning, top-side up, onto wire rack to cool.

5 Spread cold cake with fudge frosting.

Simmer water, sugar, butter, cocoa and soda until sugar dissolves.

Pour cake mixture evenly into prepared baking dish.

marble cake

preparation time 30 minutes cooking time 1 hour (plus cooling time)
serves 10

250g butter, softened
1 teaspoon vanilla extract
1¼ cups (275g) caster sugar
3 eggs
2¼ cups (335g) self-raising flour
¾ cup (180ml) milk
pink food colouring
2 tablespoons cocoa powder
1 tablespoon milk, extra

pink butter icing
90g soft butter
1 cup (160g) icing sugar
1 tablespoon milk
pink food colouring

pink butter icing
Beat butter in small bowl with electric
mixer until light and fluffy; beat in icing
sugar and milk. Tint with pink colouring.

1 Preheat oven to moderate (180°C/160°C fan-assisted). Grease deep
22cm-round cake tin; line base with baking parchment.

2 Beat butter, extract and sugar in medium bowl with electric mixer until light
and fluffy. Add eggs, one at a time, beating until combined. Using wooden
spoon, stir in flour and milk, in two batches.

3 Divide mixture evenly among three bowls; tint mixture in one bowl pink by
stirring through a few drops of colouring with a wooden spoon.

4 Using a teaspoon, blend sifted cocoa with extra milk in a cup; stir into the
second bowl of mixture.

5 Drop alternate spoonfuls of the three coloured mixtures into tin. Pull a skewer
backwards and forwards through cake mixture several times for a marbled
effect; smooth surface with metal spatula.

6 Bake, uncovered, about 1 hour. Stand cake 5 minutes before turning, top-side
up, onto wire rack to cool.

7 Spread cold cake with pink butter icing.

Stir cocoa into one third of the cake
mixture.

Drop spoonfuls of coloured mixture,
alternately, into tin.

To marble the cake, pull a skewer back
and forth through the mixture.

food colourings
There are many types of food colourings available including pastes, gels, powders and liquids. Since they all vary greatly in strength, start tinting by using only a drop or a tiny amount, then increase the amount until you get the depth of colour you desire.

tip This cake is 'amazing' because, while a runny mixture is poured into the cake tin, it is a three-layered 'pie' that emerges from the oven. The bottom layer is pastry-like because the flour and butter sink to the bottom; the centre layer is like a custard filling; and the top is slightly browned and crusty because the coconut, the lightest ingredient, floats to the top during baking.

amazing pie

preparation time 15 minutes   cooking time 45 minutes   serves 6

4 eggs
½ cup plain flour (75g)
1 cup caster sugar (220g)
1 cup desiccated coconut (90g)
125g butter, melted
300ml whipping cream
¾ cup milk (180ml)
1 tablespoon finely grated
lemon rind
¼ cup lemon juice (60ml)

1 Preheat oven to moderate. Grease straight-sided deep 19cm-square cake tin.

2 Whisk eggs in large bowl; gradually whisk in flour then remaining ingredients until mixture is well combined. Pour mixture into prepared tin.

3 Bake, uncovered, in moderate oven about 45 minutes or until browned and set. If serving warm, stand in tin for 20 minutes before cutting; if serving cold, cool in the tin to room temperature or refrigerate, covered, until serving time. Cut into 6 pieces; remove from tin using spatula. Serve dusted with sifted icing sugar and extra citrus rind, if desired, accompanied by the fruit, if you like.

coconut apricot cake

preparation time 25 minutes   cooking time 1 hour 30 minutes   serves 22

185g butter, softened
¾ cup (165g) caster sugar
3 eggs
1 cup (90g) desiccated coconut
½ cup (75g) plain flour
½ cup (75g) self-raising flour
½ cup (125ml) coconut milk
1 cup (190g) coarsely chopped dried figs
¾ cup (185g) coarsely chopped dried apricots
⅔ cup (110g) sultanas

1 Position oven shelves; preheat oven to low. Line base and side of deep 20cm-round cake tin with three thicknesses baking parchment, extending parchment 5cm above edge of tin.

2 Beat butter, sugar, eggs, coconut, flours and milk in large bowl on low speed with electric mixer until ingredients are combined. Beat on medium speed until mixture is changed in colour. Using wooden spoon, stir in fruit; spread mixture into prepared tin.

3 Bake cake in low oven about 1½ hours.

4 Cover tin tightly with foil; cool cake in tin.

tips Cover cake loosely with foil during baking if it starts to overbrown.
★ Give the cake quarter turns several times during baking if browning unevenly.
★ You can substitute dried dates for the dried figs, and glacé pineapple for either the apricots or figs.

banana cake

preparation time 35 minutes cooking time 55 minutes (plus cooling time)
serves 10

125g butter, softened
¾ cup (150g) firmly packed brown sugar
2 eggs
1½ cups (225g) self-raising flour
½ teaspoon bicarbonate of soda
1 teaspoon mixed spice
1 cup mashed banana
½ cup (120g) soured cream
¼ cup (60ml) milk

cream cheese frosting
1 cup (160g) icing sugar
250g cream cheese

Use a fork to mash ripe bananas.

Using a plastic spatula, spread mixture into prepared tin.

Spread cold cake evenly with cream cheese frosting.

1 Preheat oven to moderate (180°C/160°C fan-assisted). Grease one 15cm x 25cm loaf tin; line base with baking parchment.

2 Beat butter and sugar in small bowl with electric mixer until light and fluffy. Beat in eggs, one at a time, until combined. Transfer mixture to large bowl; using wooden spoon, stir in sifted dry ingredients, banana, sour cream and milk. Spread mixture into tin.

3 Bake cake about 50 minutes. Stand cake 5 minutes before turning, top-side up, onto wire rack to cool.

4 Spread cold cake with cream cheese frosting.

cream cheese frosting
Beat sifted icing sugar and cream cheese in small bowl, on medium speed, with electric mixer until mixture is smooth.

tip You need two large overripe bananas for this recipe because they mash easily and are the most flavourful. If the bananas you buy are not ripe enough, put them in a paper bag and keep them at room temperature for a day or two.

lumberjack cake

2 large apples (400g), peeled, cored, chopped finely
1 cup (200g) finely chopped pitted dried dates
1 teaspoon bicarbonate of soda
1 cup (250ml) boiling water
125g butter, softened
1 teaspoon vanilla essence
1 cup (220g) caster sugar
1 egg
1½ cups (225g) plain flour

topping
60g butter
½ cup (100g) firmly packed brown sugar
½ cup (125ml) milk
⅔ cup (50g) shredded coconut

preparation time 30 minutes baking time 1 hour 10 minutes serves 12

1 Position oven shelves; preheat oven to moderate. Grease deep 23cm-square cake tin; line base and sides with baking parchment.

2 Combine apple, dates and soda in large bowl, add the water, cover bowl with cling film; stand 10 minutes.

3 Meanwhile, beat butter, essence, sugar and egg in small bowl with electric mixer until light and fluffy.

4 Add creamed butter mixture to apple mixture; using wooden spoon, stir in flour well. Pour mixture into prepared tin.

5 Bake cake in moderate oven 50 minutes.

6 Remove cake carefully from oven to work top; close oven door to maintain correct oven temperature. Using metal spatula, carefully spread warm topping evenly over cake; return cake to oven, bake about 20 minutes or until topping has browned.

7 Stand cake 5 minutes then turn onto wire rack; turn cake top-side up to cool.

topping
Combine ingredients in medium saucepan; using wooden spoon, stir topping mixture over low heat until butter melts and sugar dissolves.

tips We used Granny Smith apples in this recipe, but any type of apple works just as well.
★ Standing the apple mixture for 10 minutes allows the bicarbonate of soda to start softening the dates.
★ Begin preparing the topping while cake is in oven for the first 50 minutes.
★ The topping can be prepared in a microwave oven. Combine all ingredients in a medium microwave-safe bowl; cook, uncovered, on HIGH (100%) for about 1 minute or until butter melts and sugar dissolves.

basic cookies

preparation time 20 minutes baking time 15 minutes makes 30

200g butter, softened
½ teaspoon vanilla extract
1 cup (160g) icing sugar
1 egg
1¾ cups (260g) plain flour
½ teaspoon bicarbonate of soda

1 Preheat oven to moderately low (170°C/150°C fan-assisted). Grease two baking trays; line with baking parchment.

2 Beat butter, extract, sifted icing sugar and egg in small bowl with electric mixer until light and fluffy. Transfer to medium bowl; stir in sifted flour and soda, in two batches.

3 Roll level tablespoons of dough into balls; place on trays 3cm apart. Bake about 15 minutes; cool cookies on trays.

variations

cranberry and coconut cookies

Stir ½ cup (65g) dried cranberries and ½ cup (40g) shredded coconut into basic cookie mixture before flour and soda are added.

choc chip cookies

Stir ½ cup (95g) dark chocolate chips into basic cookie mixture before flour and soda are added. Roll level tablespoons of dough into balls then roll balls in a mixture of 1 tablespoon caster sugar, 2 teaspoons ground nutmeg and 2 teaspoons ground cinnamon.

pear and ginger cookies

Stir ¼ cup (35g) finely chopped dried pears, ¼ cup (55g) coarsely chopped glacé ginger and ½ cup (45g) rolled oats into basic cookie mixture before flour and soda are added.

brown sugar and pecan cookies

Substitute 1 cup (220g) firmly packed brown sugar for the icing sugar in the basic cookie mixture. Stir ½ cup (60g) coarsely chopped pecans into basic cookie mixture before flour and soda are added.

chunky chocolate-chip cookies

preparation time 20 minutes   cooking time 10 minutes   makes 36

125g butter, chopped
1 teaspoon vanilla extract
1¼ cups (275g) firmly packed brown sugar
1 egg
1 cup (150g) plain flour
¼ cup (35g) self-raising flour
½ teaspoon bicarbonate of soda
⅓ cup (35g) cocoa powder
½ cup (100g) peanut M&M's
⅓ cup (70g) mini M&M's
½ cup (75g) milk chocolate Buttons

Beat the butter, extract, sugar and egg in small bowl until smooth.

1 Preheat oven to moderate. Lightly grease two baking trays.

2 Beat butter, extract, sugar and egg in small bowl with electric mixer until smooth (do not overmix). Transfer to large bowl; mix in sifted combined dry ingredients then all chocolates.

3 Drop level tablespoons of the mixture onto prepared trays, allowing 5cm between each cookie; bake, uncovered, in moderate oven about 10 minutes. Stand cookies 5 minutes; transfer to wire rack to cool.

Drop level tablespoons of the mixture, 5cm apart, onto trays.

crunchy muesli cookies

preparation time **15 minutes**   cooking time **25 minutes**   makes **36**

1 cup (90g) rolled oats
1 cup (150g) plain flour
1 cup (220g) caster sugar
2 teaspoons ground cinnamon
¼ cup (35g) dried cranberries
⅓ cup (55g) finely chopped dried apricots
½ cup (70g) slivered almonds
125g butter
2 tablespoons golden syrup
½ teaspoon bicarbonate of soda
1 tablespoon boiling water

1 Preheat oven to low (150°C/130°C fan-assisted). Grease two baking trays; line with baking parchment.

2 Combine oats, flour, sugar, cinnamon, dried fruit and nuts in large bowl.

3 Melt butter with golden syrup in small saucepan over low heat; add combined soda and the boiling water. Stir warm butter mixture into dry ingredients.

4 Roll level tablespoons of mixture into balls, place on trays 5cm apart; flatten with hand. Bake about 20 minutes; cool cookies on trays.

turkish delight rocky road

preparation time 15 minutes cooking time 5 minutes (plus refrigeration time)
makes 28

400g white eating chocolate, chopped coarsely
200g raspberry and vanilla marshmallows, chopped coarsely
200g turkish delight, chopped finely
¾ cup (110g) toasted macadamias, chopped coarsely

1 Line two 8cm x 25cm shallow cake tins with baking parchment, extending parchment 2cm over all sides of tins.

2 Stir chocolate in medium heatproof bowl over medium saucepan of simmering water until smooth; cool 2 minutes.

3 Meanwhile, combine remaining ingredients in large bowl. Working quickly, stir in chocolate; spread mixture into tins. Refrigerate until set; cut into 1cm slices.

did you know?

turkish delight
According to legend, turkish delight was developed by an Ottoman sultan to appeal to the sweet tooth of the hundreds of wives in his harem. The recipe, virtually unchanged for the past 500 years, proved an overwhelming success and it has become a sweet enjoyed around the world.

special occasions

Birthdays, Christmas, Easter – it's always exciting to celebrate a special occasion, and nothing says special occasion more than a spectacular cake or plate of fun cookies!

chocolate birthday cake

preparation time 30 minutes cooking time 1 hour (plus cooling time)
serves 8

125g butter, softened
1 teaspoon vanilla extract
1 cup (220g) caster sugar
2 eggs
⅔ cup (160ml) water
1⅓ cups (200g) self-raising flour
½ cup (50g) cocoa powder
white eating chocolate, for decoration
dark eating chocolate, for decoration

chocolate icing
60g butter, softened
1½ cups (240g) icing sugar
2 tablespoons cocoa powder
2 tablespoons milk

1 Preheat oven to moderate (180°C/160°C fan-assisted). Grease deep 20cm-round cake tin; line base with baking parchment.

2 Combine butter, extract, sugar, eggs, the water and sifted flour and cocoa powder in medium bowl; beat on low speed with electric mixer until ingredients are combined.

3 Increase speed to medium; beat about 4 minutes or until mixture is smooth and paler in colour. Pour mixture into tin.

4 Bake, uncovered, about 1 hour. Stand cake in tin 5 minutes before turning, top-side up, onto a wire rack to cool.

5 Spread cold cake with chocolate icing.

6 Using vegetable peeler, peel sides of both chocolates to create curls. Sprinkle cake with chocolate curls.

chocolate icing
Beat butter in small bowl with electric mixer until light and fluffy. Gradually beat in sifted icing sugar and cocoa with the milk.

Beat mixture on medium speed until paler in colour and smooth.

Use a spatula to scrape mixture evenly into prepared pan.

Peel sides of chocolate with vegetable peeler to make curls.

valentine chocolate hearts

preparation time 20 minutes   cooking time 30 minutes (plus cooling time)
makes 20

175g butter
270g dark chocolate, chopped
coarsely
½ cup (110g) firmly packed
brown sugar
¾ cup (180ml) water
¾ cup (110g) plain flour
¼ cup (35g) self-raising flour
1 egg
paper hearts
cocoa powder, for dusting
icing sugar, for dusting

tip Make your own paper hearts cut out from baking parchment, or you can place a smaller heart-shaped cutter, covered with cling film, on each cake before dusting.

1 Preheat oven to low (150°C/130°C fan-assisted). Grease 26cm x 32cm Swiss roll tin; line base and sides with two layers of baking parchment, extending parchment 3cm above sides.

2 Place butter, chocolate, brown sugar and the water in medium saucepan. Stir over low heat until melted. Transfer to large bowl; cool 10 minutes.

3 Add flours and egg to chocolate mixture; whisk until smooth, pour into tin.

4 Bake, uncovered, about 20 minutes; cool cake in tin.

5 Turn cake onto board; remove lining parchment. Using a 5cm heart cutter, cut heart shapes from cake. Place paper hearts in centre of cake, dust half the little cakes with sifted cocoa and half with sifted icing sugar; carefully remove paper hearts.

Pour mixture evenly into prepared tin.

Use a cutter to cut hearts.

Dust hearts with icing sugar.

chocolate easter cake

preparation time 30 minutes cooking time 1 hour 10 minutes (plus cooling time) serves 10

½ cup (50g) cocoa powder
½ cup (125ml) boiling water
185g butter
1½ cups (330g) firmly packed brown sugar
3 eggs
1½ cups (225g) self-raising flour
½ cup (75g) plain flour
¼ teaspoon bicarbonate of soda
¾ cup (180m) milk
2 teaspoons vanilla extract
150g small milk chocolate Easter eggs
coloured cake decorations

milk chocolate icing
400g milk eating chocolate, chopped
⅔ cup (160ml) whipping cream

1 Preheat oven to moderately low (170°C/ 150°C fan-assisted). Grease deep 22cm-round cake tin; line base with baking parchment.

2 Combine cocoa powder and the water in small bowl; whisk until smooth. Let cool.

3 Beat butter and sugar in small bowl with electric mixer until light and fluffy. Add eggs, one at a time, beating until combined between additions. Transfer mixture to large bowl.

4 Stir in sifted flours and soda, then milk, extract and cocoa mixture. Pour mixture into tin.

5 Bake, uncovered, about 1 hour 10 minutes. Stand 10 minutes before turning, top-side up, onto wire rack to cool.

6 Spread milk chocolate icing over top and side of cold cake, decorate with chocolate eggs and coloured decorations.

milk chocolate icing
Combine chocolate and cream in small saucepan, stir over very low heat until smooth. Transfer to medium bowl. Refrigerate, stirring frequently, until icing is a spreadable consistency.

Mix ingredients together in a large bowl.

Pour mixture into pan, scraping out bowl with a rubber spatula.

Using a metal spatula, spread icing evenly over cake.

hallow'een cake

5 x 340g packets chocolate cake mix
30cm x 40cm cake board

chocolate buttercream

375g butter, softened
4½ cups (720g) icing sugar
6 tablespoons milk
¼ cup (25g) cocoa powder
brown food colouring

black glacé icing

1 cup (160g) icing sugar
1 tablespoon water
black food colouring

decorations

2 tablespoons shredded coconut
green food colouring
3 bamboo skewers
2 toothpicks
fruit bat jellies
spearmint leaves
green, red and yellow jelly snakes
red and yellow boiled lollies
50g Toblerone chocolate bar
80g milk chocolate sultanas

preparation time 45 minutes **cooking time** 1¼ hours (plus cooling time) **serves** 10

1 Preheat oven to moderate (180°C/160°C fan-assisted). Grease and line deep 23cm-square cake tin and 20cm x 30cm baking tin; grease 1.75-litre (7-cup) pudding basin.

2 Make two of the packet cakes according to the directions; pour into square cake tin. Make remaining packet cakes; pour 4½ cups of mixture into pudding basin, pour remaining mixture into baking tin. Bake square cake about 1¼ hours; bake basin cake about 50 minutes and cake in baking tin about 40 minutes. Stand cakes 10 minutes before turning onto wire racks to cool.

3 Using serrated knife, level tops of all cakes. Using picture as a guide, cut wall from square cake and cut base from rectangular cake. Carve out mouth of cave from pudding cake.

4 Make black glacé icing. Pour black glacé icing into cave. Turn cake to evenly coat inside of cave. Stand until set.

5 Make buttercream. Place base, cut-side down, on cake board; spread with buttercream. Spread buttercream all over wall cake; stand wall behind base so that the wall is positioned to one end of the base. Slice back of pudding cake (cave) so it fits flat against the wall. Spread buttercream over outside of cave; position on top of base, against the wall. Smooth buttercream to cover joins.

6 Combine coconut with green colouring in small plastic bag, rub together until coconut is coloured; sprinkle over cake where you are going to place the vines. Position green snakes and leaves to resemble vines.

7 Dab a drop of brown colouring onto absorbent paper, wipe along length of bamboo skewers and toothpicks to colour. Push skewers and toothpicks into bat lollies. Using small paintbrush, paint front of bat lollies with black food colouring; position in and around cave to suggest flying bats.

8 Using picture as a guide, decorate cake with remaining lollies to complete bat cave.

chocolate buttercream

Beat butter in large bowl with electric mixer until as white as possible. Gradually beat in half the sifted icing sugar, milk, then remaining icing sugar. Beat sifted cocoa and brown colouring into buttercream.

black glacé icing

Sift icing sugar into small heatproof bowl; stir in the water and colouring. Stir over small saucepan of simmering water until icing is spreadable.

Cut away some of the front of the cake to form cave mouth; pour black glacé icing inside to coat cave mouth.

christmas gingerbread biscuits

125g butter, softened
½ cup (110g) firmly packed brown sugar
½ cup (125ml) treacle
1 egg yolk
2½ cups (375g) plain flour
1 tablespoon ground ginger
1 teaspoon mixed spice
1 teaspoon bicarbonate of soda
silver cake decorations

royal icing
2 egg whites
3 cups (480g) icing sugar
variety of food colourings

preparation time 30 minutes (plus refrigeration time)
cooking time 10 minutes per tray   makes 40

1 Beat butter and sugar in small bowl with electric mixer until light and fluffy; beat in treacle and egg yolk. Transfer mixture to large bowl, stir in sifted dry ingredients. Knead dough on lightly floured surface until smooth; cover, refrigerate 1 hour.

2 Preheat oven to moderate (180°C/160°C fan-assisted).

3 Roll dough between sheets of baking paper until 4mm thick. Cut shapes from dough using Christmas cutters. Make a small hole in the top of each biscuit for threading through ribbon, if desired. Place shapes 3cm apart on greased oven trays.

4 Bake, uncovered, about 10 minutes or until browned lightly (time depends on the size of the shapes). Transfer shapes to wire racks to cool. Spread or pipe royal icing onto cold biscuits; decorate with cachous.

royal icing
Beat egg whites in small bowl with electric mixer until soft peaks form. Gradually add sifted icing sugar, beat well between additions. Divide icing into several small bowls, tint each bowl of icing with colourings, as desired. Keep icing tightly covered with cling film at all times to prevent it from drying out.

tips For bold icing colours, we used powdered food colourings, available from cake decorating shops and some health food stores. Mixing the powder with a small amount of hot water, before stirring into the icing, gives a better result; liquid colourings can be used for pale colours.
★ Decorated gingerbread shapes can be made two weeks ahead; store in an airtight container.

stained-glass christmas cookies

preparation time 1 hour (plus refrigeration time) cooking time 1 hou (plus cooling time) makes 36

250g butter, softened
2 teaspoons finely grated lemon rind
½ teaspoon almond essence
¾ cup (165g) caster sugar
1 egg
1 tablespoon water
2¼ cups (335g) plain flour
90g individually wrapped sugar-free fruit drops, assorted colours

1 Beat butter, rind, essence, sugar, egg and the water in small bowl with electric mixer until smooth (do not overbeat). Transfer to large bowl; stir in sifted flour. Knead dough on floured surface until smooth, cover with cling film; refrigerate 30 minutes.

2 Preheat oven to moderate (180°C/160°C fan-assisted). Line two baking trays with baking parchment.

3 Using a rolling pin, gently tap the wrapped sweets to crush them slightly. Unwrap lollies; separate by colour into small bowls.

4 Roll dough between sheets of baking parchment until 4mm thick. Cut shapes from dough using medium-sized cookie cutters; use very small cookie cutters to cut out the centre of each cookie to make a window. Make a small hole in the top of each biscuit for threading through ribbon, if desired.

5 Place cookies on oven trays; bake, uncovered, 5 minutes. Remove trays from oven; fill the centre of each biscuit with a few of the same-coloured crushed sweets. Return to oven for 5 minutes or until browned lightly. Cool cookies on baking trays.

Lightly tap coloured sweets with a rolling pin to make your 'glass'.

Roll dough out to about 4mm thick, then cut into different shapes with biscuit cutters.

Fill cut-out centre of each biscuit with crushed coloured sweets for a stained-glass effect.

christmas cake

preparation time 30 minutes   cooking time 3 hours (plus cooling time)
serves 36

250g butter, softened
1¼ cups (275g) firmly packed brown sugar
4 eggs
2 tablespoons orange marmalade
1.5kg (7½ cups) mixed dried fruit
1½ cups (225g) plain flour
½ cup (75g) self-raising flour
2 teaspoons mixed spice
½ cup (125ml) orange juice
¼ cup (40g) blanched whole almonds

Add flours and spice to mix with apple juice.

Spread mixture evenly into prepared pan.

Level surface of cake mixture with wet metal spatula.

1 Preheat oven to slow (150°C/130°C fan-assisted). Line base and sides of deep 19cm-square cake tin with three thicknesses of baking parchment, bringing parchment 5cm above sides of tin.

2 Beat butter and sugar in small bowl with electric mixer until just combined. Beat in eggs, one at a time, until just combined between additions. Mixture may curdle at this point, but will come together later.

3 Scrape mixture into large bowl; add marmalade and fruit, mix thoroughly.

4 Sift flours and spice over mixture; add juice, mix well. Drop dollops of mixture into corners of tin to hold baking parchment in position; spread remaining mixture into tin.

5 Drop cake tin from a height of about 15cm onto work top to settle mixture into tin and to break any large air bubbles. Level surface of cake mixture with wet metal spatula; decorate top with almonds.

tips Have the butter and eggs at room temperature before you use them to help prevent the mixture from curdling.
★ Cover cake loosely with foil during baking if it starts to overbrown. Give the cake quarter turns several times during baking to avoid uneven browning.
★ Covered cake in tin will go from oven to room temperature in about 24 hours. Remove cake from tin by turning cake upside down onto work top and carefully peeling lining paper away from sides but leaving base paper in place. Wrap cake tightly in cling film to keep airtight, then wrap in foil.

party food

These are some cool ideas for adults to make for parties for friends and family. If your party is at home or off-site, these goodies are different and so easy to eat, they will melt off the plates. Don't forget to keep sandwiches covered with a damp cloth until serving and find a variety of bowls or plates to serve them from.

tip Spring rolls can be cooked one day ahead; keep, covered, in the refrigerator. Reheat rolls, in single layer, on baking trays, covered loosely with foil, in oven (180°C/160°C fan-assisted) for about 10 minutes.

chicken spring rolls

preparation time 15 minutes (plus cooling time) cooking time 30 minutes
makes 16

16 x 12.5cm spring roll wrappers
1 egg, beaten lightly
vegetable oil, for deep-frying

filling
2 teaspoons vegetable oil
150g minced chicken
1 clove garlic, crushed
1cm piece fresh ginger (5g), grated
2 spring onions, chopped finely
1 small carrot (70g), grated finely
½ cup (40g) coarsely chopped beansprouts
1 tablespoon oyster sauce

1 Make filling.

2 Place a level tablespoon of filling across edge of each wrapper; brush edges with egg, roll to enclose filling, folding in ends.

3 Deep-fry spring rolls, in batches, in hot oil until browned lightly; drain on absorbent paper.

4 Serve rolls with sweet chilli sauce.

filling
Heat oil in medium frying pan; stir-fry chicken, garlic and ginger until chicken is browned lightly. Remove from heat, stir in onion, carrot, sprouts and sauce; cool.

mini beef meatballs

preparation time 25 minutes   cooking time 20 minutes   makes 55

1kg minced beef
I cup (70g) stale breadcrumbs
1/2 cup (40g) coarsely grated parmesan cheese
2 cloves garlic, crushed
2 spring onions, sliced thinly
1 tablespoon worcestershire sauce
2 tablespoons barbecue sauce
2 tablespoons olive oil

1 Combine beef, breadcrumbs, cheese, garlic, onion and sauces in large bowl; shape level tablespoons of mixture into balls.

2 Heat oil in large frying pan; cook meatballs, in batches, until cooked. Drain on absorbent paper.

3 Serve meatballs with tomato sauce.

tips Meatballs can be cooked one day ahead; keep, covered, in refrigerator. Reheat meatballs, in single layer, on baking trays, covered loosely with foil, in oven (180°C/160°C fan-assisted) for about 10 minutes.
★ Uncooked meatballs can be frozen between layers of freezer wrap for up to three months; thaw in refrigerator for 12 hours or overnight before cooking as per recipe.

party pizzas with 3 toppings

preparation time 20 minutes   cooking time 20 minutes   makes 12

1 cup (280g) tomato paste
12 x 225g mini pizza bases

hawaiian style
1½ cups (150g) pizza cheese
150g ham, chopped coarsely
1 cup (180g) drained canned pineapple pieces

toppings

each of the toppings makes enough for four pizza bases

hawaiian style

Sprinkle 1 cup of the cheese over four bases. Top with ham, pineapple then remaining cheese.

vegetarian

Sprinkle 1 cup of the cheese over four bases. Top with capsicum, mushrooms, olives and tomato then remaining cheese.

chicken, broccoli and sweet chilli

Drop broccoli into small saucepan of boiling water; return to a boil, drain. Sprinkle 1 cup of the cheese over four bases. Top with chicken and remaining cheese. Serve sprinkled with broccoli and sauce.

vegetarian
1½ cups (150g) pizza cheese
½ cup (120g) coarsely chopped char-grilled green pepper
50g button mushrooms, sliced thinly
¼ cup (30g) pitted black olives, sliced thinly
⅓ cup (50g) drained semi-dried tomatoes, chopped coarsely

chicken, broccoli and sweet chilli
1 cup (85g) small broccoli florets
1½ cups (150g) pizza cheese
2 cups (320g) shredded cooked chicken
¼ cup (60ml) sweet chilli sauce

1 Preheat oven to 200°C/180°C fan-assisted.

2 Spread 1 tablespoon of the tomato paste over each pizza base. Place bases on oven trays; sprinkle with toppings, as instructed, below. Bake about 20 minutes or until browned.

bacon-wrapped chicken patties

preparation time 45 minutes (plus freezing time) cooking time 15 minutes
makes 24

400g minced chicken
1 tablespoon finely chopped chives
2 tablespoons finely chopped fresh flat-leaf parsley
1 trimmed celery stalk (100g), chopped finely
1 clove garlic, crushed
1 teaspoon finely grated lemon rind
2 tablespoons packaged breadcrumbs
¼ cup (20g) finely grated parmesan cheese
¼ cup (75g) mayonnaise
3 thin rindless rashers bacon (90g)

1 Combine chicken, herbs, celery, garlic, rind, breadcrumbs, cheese and mayonnaise in medium bowl. Shape rounded tablespoons of mixture into patties; place on baking-parchment-lined tray. Freeze 30 minutes.

2 Meanwhile, cut each bacon rasher in half crossways then cut each half into four lengthways strips. Wrap a strip of bacon around each patty; secure with toothpicks.

3 Cook patties in heated oiled large frying pan until browned all over and cooked through. Remove toothpicks before serving.

tips Uncooked patties can be prepared one day ahead; keep, covered, in refrigerator. Cook patties as per recipe.
★ Uncooked patties can be frozen between layers of freezer wrap for up to three months; thaw in refrigerator for 12 hours or overnight before cooking as per recipe.

tips Chicken can be crumbed one day ahead; keep, covered, in refrigerator.
★ Cook chicken just before serving.

cheesy chicken strips

preparation time 15 minutes cooking time 25 minutes serves 12

1kg small chicken tenderloins, halved lengthways
½ cup (75g) plain flour
2 eggs
¼ cup (60ml) milk
1½ cups (240g) cornflake crumbs
½ cup (40g) finely grated parmesan cheese
cooking-oil spray

1 Preheat oven to 200°C /180°C fan-assisted.

2 Coat chicken in flour; shake away excess. Dip chicken in combined egg and milk; coat in combined crumbs and cheese.

3 Place chicken, in single layer, on wire rack over oven tray; spray with oil. Cook about 25 minutes or until cooked through.

4 Serve chicken strips with tomato sauce.

mini chicken pies

preparation time 40 minutes (plus cooling time) cooking time 45 minutes
makes 24

200g chicken breast fillet
1½ cups (375ml) chicken stock
25g butter
1 medium leek (350g), sliced thinly
1 trimmed celery stalk (100g),
chopped finely
1 tablespoon plain flour
1 teaspoon dijon mustard
1 tablespoon coarsely chopped
fresh flat-leaf parsley
6 sheets ready-rolled puff pastry
1 egg

1 Combine chicken and stock in small saucepan; simmer, covered, about 10 minutes or until chicken is cooked through. Remove from heat; cool chicken in stock to room temperature. Remove chicken; chop finely. Reserve ¾ cup of the stock.

2 Melt butter in same saucepan, add leek and celery; cook, stirring, until soft. Stir in flour and mustard. Gradually stir in reserved stock; stir over heat until mixture boils and thickens. Add chicken and parsley. Cool.

3 Preheat oven to 220°C/200°C fan-assisted. Oil two 12-hole (⅓-cup/80ml) muffin trays.

4 Cut 24 x 7cm rounds from pastry sheets; press rounds into each tray hole. Divide chicken mixture among pastry cases; brush cases with egg. Cut out 24 x 6cm rounds from remaining pastry; position on top of pastry cases, press edges with fork to seal. Cut a small cross in top of each lid. Bake about 25 minutes or until browned. Stand 10 minutes before serving with tomato ketchup.

tips Pies can be cooked one day ahead; keep, covered, in refrigerator.
★ Reheat pies in a single layer on baking trays, covered loosely with foil, in moderate oven (180°C/160°C fan-assisted) for about 10 minutes.
★ Uncooked pies can be frozen between layers of freezer wrap for up to three months; thaw in refrigerator for 12 hours or overnight before cooking as per recipe.

tips Twists can be cooked up to two days ahead; store in an airtight container. Serve twists at room temperature or reheat, in single layer, on baking trays, covered loosely with foil, in oven (180°C/160°C fan-assisted) for about 10 minutes.
★ Uncooked twists can be frozen between layers of freezer wrap for up to three months. Cook twists from frozen state, as per recipe.

cheese twists

preparation time **15 minutes** cooking time **10 minutes** makes **20**

2 sheets ready-rolled puff pastry
1 tablespoon tomato sauce
1 cup (100g) pizza cheese
1 tablespoon milk

1 Preheat oven to 220°C/200°C fan-assisted. Line oven trays with baking parchment.

2 Spread one piece of pastry with tomato sauce; sprinkle with cheese. Top with remaining pastry; press down firmly.

3 Cut pastry into 20 strips. Twist strips, place 2cm apart on trays; brush with milk. Bake about 10 minutes or until browned lightly. Serve warm or at room temperature.

party wedges

preparation time 10 minutes   cooking time 40 minutes   serves 10

5 large oval-shaped potatoes (1.5kg)
cooking-oil spray

1 Preheat oven to 200°C/180°C fan-assisted. Line baking tray with baking parchment.

2 Halve potatoes lengthways; cut each half into three wedges. Boil or steam wedges, covered, 5 minutes; drain.

3 Place wedges on tray; spray with oil. Cook about 30 minutes or until browned, turning occasionally.

tips Wedges can be prepared up to three hours ahead; bake just before serving.
★ We used desiree potatoes for this recipe.

heart-shaped hamwiches

preparation time 30 minutes makes 18

18 slices white bread
⅓ cup (80g) spreadable cream cheese
100g wafer-thin ham

1 Using 7.5cm heart cutter, cut two hearts from each slice of bread. Using 4cm heart cutter, cut out a smaller heart from the centre of half the large hearts.

2 Spread one side of the large uncut hearts with some of the cream cheese; top with ham. Spread the remaining cream cheese on one side of the remaining hearts; place on top of ham.

tips You need a loaf of the larger-sized bread (slices measure 12cm across).

★ The little cut-out hearts can be used to make fairy bread or sandwiched with a cut-out heart of sliced cheese, held together with a toothpick and grilled until browned.

★ Use heart cutter to cut-out heart shapes from ham for a really neat fit.

★ Sandwiches can be made three hours ahead; keep covered in refrigerator.

baby BLTs

preparation time 15 minutes
cooking time 15 minutes serves 12

12 'bake at home' dinner rolls
6 rindless bacon rashers (390g)
⅓ cup (100g) mayonnaise
2 small tomatoes (180g),
sliced thinly
1 gem lettuce, leaves separated

1 Preheat oven to 180°C/160°C fan-assisted.

2 Place bread rolls on oven tray, bake 5 minutes. Split rolls in half almost all the way through.

3 Meanwhile, cut bacon in half crossways; cook bacon in heated large frying pan until crisp. Drain on absorbent paper.

4 Just before serving, spread mayonnaise inside rolls; fill rolls with bacon, lettuce and tomato.

party nachos

preparation time 15 minutes cooking time 10 minutes serves 10

420g can mexican-style beans, rinsed, drained
290g can kidney beans, rinsed, drained, mashed
2 tablespoons tomato paste
¼ cup (60ml) water
230g packet plain corn chips
1½ cups (180g) coarsely grated cheddar cheese
1 large avocado (320g)
1 tablespoon lemon juice
1 small red onion (100g), chopped finely
1 large tomato (220g), chopped finely
½ cup (120g) soured cream
2 tablespoons fresh coriander leaves

1 Preheat oven to 200°C/180°C fan-assisted.

2 Heat combined beans, paste and the water, stirring, in large frying pan. Cover; keep warm.

3 Place corn chips in individual ovenproof dishes; sprinkle with cheese. Bake, in oven, about 5 minutes or until cheese melts.

4 Meanwhile, mash avocado in small bowl; stir in juice, onion and tomato.

5 Top heated corn chips with bean mixture, avocado mixture and soured cream; sprinkle nachos with coriander, and cracked black pepper, if you like.

tips Party nachos are best made just before serving.
★ You can prepare nachos in large ovenproof dish, rather than individual dishes, if you prefer.

tips Rice paper rolls can be made three hours ahead; cover with slightly damp cloth then foil or cling film and keep in refrigerator.
★ Chinese cabbage is elongated in shape with pale green, crinkly leaves. It is the most commonly used cabbage in South-East Asia, and is available from Asian grocery stores and most major supermarkets.

vegetable rice paper rolls

preparation time 30 minutes   makes 24

1 large carrot (180g), grated coarsely
2 trimmed celery stalks (200g), chopped finely
150g chinese cabbage, shredded finely
2 teaspoons fish sauce
2 teaspoons brown sugar
1 tablespoon lemon juice
24 x 17cm-square rice paper sheets
24 fresh mint leaves

1 Combine carrot, celery, chinese cabbage, sauce, sugar and juice in medium size bowl.

2 Place 1 sheet of rice paper in medium bowl of warm water until just softened; lift sheet carefully from water, place on tea-towel-covered board.

3 Place 1 level tablespoon of vegetable mixture across edge of sheet; top with mint leaf. Roll to enclose filling, folding in ends. Repeat with remaining rice paper sheets, vegetable mixture and mint leaves. Serve with sweet chilli sauce.

tips Canapés can be made an hour ahead; keep, covered, in refrigerator.
★ Canapés are not suitable to freeze.
★ Instead of piping the cream cheese onto the canapés, just dollop on using a teaspoon.

80g packet mini toasts

ham and cheese
2 tablespoons cheese spread
2 slices (30g) thin ham, cut into
1.5cm strips
1 teaspoon finely chopped fresh
flat-leaf parsley

hummus and carrot
2 tablespoons hummus
2 tablespoons finely grated carrot
12 coriander leaves

cream cheese and sweet chilli
¼ cup (90g) spreadable cream
cheese, softened
2 teaspoons finely chopped fresh
flat-leaf parsley
1 tablespoon sweet chilli sauce

canapés with 3 toppings

preparation time 25 minutes   makes 36

ham and cheese
Spread most of the cheese over 12 mini toasts; top with rolled ham, then a small dollop of remaining cheese, sprinkle with parsley.

hummus and carrot
Spread hummus over 12 mini toasts; top with carrot then coriander.

cream cheese and sweet chilli
Combine cream cheese and parsley in small bowl. Spoon mixture into piping bag fitted with a medium plain tube; pipe cream cheese mixture on remaining toasts. Drizzle each with sweet chilli sauce.

chicken and vegetable rolls

preparation time 15 minutes cooking time 30 minutes makes 48

500g minced chicken
1 clove garlic, crushed
1 medium brown onion (150g),
chopped finely
1 medium carrot (120g), grated
finely
100g green beans, trimmed,
chopped finely
125g can creamed sweetcorn
1 egg
⅓ cup (25g) stale breadcrumbs
1 tablespoon tomato sauce
4 sheets ready-rolled puff pastry
1 egg, extra

1 Preheat oven to 200°C/180°C fan-assisted. Line baking trays with baking parchment.

2 Combine mince, garlic, onion, carrot, beans, sweetcorn, egg, breadcrumbs and sauce in medium bowl.

3 Cut pastry sheets in half lengthways. Spoon or pipe mince mixture down centre of each pastry piece. Turn one long side of pastry over mince mixture; brush pastry flap with extra egg. Turn other long side of pastry over to enclose mince mixture.

4 Cut each roll into six pieces. Place rolls, seam-side down, on trays; brush with egg. Make two cuts in top of each roll; bake about 30 minutes or until browned.

5 Stand 10 minutes before serving with tomato sauce.

tips Use a large piping bag fitted with a large plain tube to pipe mince mixture onto pastry.
★ Rolls can be cooked one day ahead; keep, covered, in refrigerator. Reheat rolls in single layer on baking trays, covered loosely with foil in oven (180°C/160°C fan-assisted) for about 15 minutes.

butterfly fairy bread

preparation time 15 minutes   makes 36

12 large slices white bread
60g soft butter
6cm butterfly cutter
18 candy sticks
½ cup hundreds and thousands

1 Spread butter on one side of each bread slice. Using butterfly cutter, cut out three butterflies from each slice.

2 Cut candy sticks in half; place one piece of candy stick in centre of each butterfly.

3 Sprinkle hundreds and thousands into small shallow dish; gently press each butterfly, buttered-side down, into hundreds and thousands. Place on serving plate.

tips Butterfly fairy bread can be made up to three hours ahead of serving; keep covered.
★ Fruit is best dipped on the day of serving. If weather is hot, refrigerate dipped fruit.

chocolate-dipped fruit

preparation time 15 minutes (plus standing time)   makes 30

2 medium bananas (400g), sliced thickly
250g strawberries
3 apricots (150g), quartered
185g milk chocolate, melted

1 Line baking tray with baking parchment.

2 Dip fruit, one piece at a time, into chocolate to coat about half of each piece of fruit. Place fruit, in single layer, on tray; allow to set at room temperature.

chewy chocolate slice

preparation time 15 minutes (plus cooling time) cooking time 25 minutes
makes 30

tip Slice can be made one week ahead; store in an airtight container at room temperature.

125g butter, melted
1 cup (220g) firmly packed brown sugar
1 egg
1 teaspoon vanilla extract
½ cup (75g) plain flour
¼ cup (35g) self-raising flour
2 tablespoons cocoa powder
½ cup (40g) desiccated coconut
1 tablespoon shredded coconut

chocolate icing
1 cup (160g) icing sugar
2 tablespoons cocoa powder
10g butter
1 tablespoon hot water

1 Preheat oven to 180°C/160°C fan-assisted. Grease 19cm x 29cm shallow baking tin; line base and two long sides with baking parchment, extending parchment 5cm above edges.

2 Combine butter, sugar, egg and extract in medium bowl. Stir in sifted flours and cocoa then desiccated coconut.

3 Spread mixture over base of tin. Bake about 25 minutes or until firm.

4 Meanwhile, make chocolate icing.

5 Spread hot slice with chocolate icing; sprinkle with shredded coconut, cool. Cut into 15 squares; cut squares into triangles.

chocolate icing
Sift icing sugar and cocoa into small bowl; add butter and the water, stir until smooth.

candied popcorn

preparation time 5 minutes (plus cooling time) cooking time 25 minutes
makes 6 cups

2 tablespoons vegetable oil
½ cup (110g) popping corn
2 cups (440g) caster sugar
1 cup (250ml) water
½ teaspoon pink food colouring

tip Candied popcorn can be made two days ahead; store in an airtight container.

1 Heat oil in large heavy-based saucepan; cook corn over high heat, covered with a tight-fitting lid, shaking pan occasionally, until popping stops. Transfer to large bowl.

2 Combine sugar, the water and colouring in medium heavy-based frying pan; stir over heat, without boiling, until sugar is dissolved. Bring to a boil; boil, uncovered, about 15 minutes or until a teaspoon of mixture cracks when dropped into a glass of cold water.

3 Remove pan from heat; when bubbles subside, add popcorn, stir to coat with toffee mixture.

4 When popcorn mixture has candied, spread onto foil-lined oven tray and allow to cool.

honey joys

preparation time 10 minutes (plus standing time) cooking time 10 minutes
makes 24

75g butter
⅓ cup (115g) honey
1 tablespoon caster sugar
5 cups (200g) cornflakes

1 Preheat oven to 180°C/160°C fan-assisted. Line two 12-hole
(⅓-cup/80ml) muffin trays with paper cases.

2 Combine butter, honey and sugar in small saucepan; stir over heat
until smooth.

3 Place cornflakes in large bowl, add butter mixture; stir until cornflakes
are well coated.

4 Divide cornflake mixture among cases; bake 8 minutes. Stand 15 minutes
or until firm.

tips Honey joys can be made one day ahead; store in an airtight container.
★ You can use different cereals in place of the cornflakes – try Rice Krispies or popcorn.

toffee-on-a-stick

preparation time 10 minutes (plus standing time) cooking time 20 minutes
makes 12

6 wooden ice-lolly sticks
1½ cups (330g) caster sugar
½ cup (125ml) water
1 tablespoon malt vinegar
hundreds and thousands

1 Grease 12-hole (1-tablespoon/20ml) mini muffin tray. Cut ice-lolly sticks in half crossways.

2 Combine sugar, the water and vinegar in medium heavy-based saucepan. Stir over heat, without boiling, until sugar is dissolved.

3 Bring mixture to a boil; boil, uncovered, without stirring, about 15 minutes or until a small amount of sugar syrup 'cracks' when dropped into a cup of cold water.

4 Remove from heat; allow bubbles to subside. Pour toffee mixture into tray holes; sprinkle with hundred and thousands.

5 Stand toffees about 10 minutes; place sticks, cut-side down, into centre of toffees. Stand toffees at room temperature until set.

tips For easy pouring, use a saucepan with a pouring lip, or carefully transfer the hot toffee to a heatproof jug.
★ Toffee can be made two days ahead; store, in single layer, in an airtight container.
★ Do not stir mixture when boiling or it will crystallise.

tip rocky road can be made one week ahead; store in an airtight container. Store in refrigerator if weather is hot.

white chocolate rocky road

preparation time 15 minutes (plus refrigeration time) **makes** 24

½ cup (150g) raspberry jelly sweets, chopped coarsely
2 tablespoons desiccated coconut
100g packet mini marshmallows
375g white eating chocolate, melted

1 Line two 12-hole (1-tablespoon/20ml) mini muffin trays with paper cases.

2 Combine raspberry fruit drops, coconut and marshmallows in medium bowl.

3 Pour chocolate into small plastic bag; snip corner to make piping bag. Pipe enough chocolate into each case to cover base.

4 Press raspberry mixture into paper cases. Pipe remaining chocolate over raspberry mixture. Refrigerate until chocolate has set.

coconut truffles

preparation time 40 minutes (plus refrigeration time) cooking time 5 minutes
makes 30

½ cup (125ml) coconut cream
2 teaspoons finely grated lime rind
2 teaspoons finely grated lemon rind
360g white eating chocolate, chopped coarsely
1¼ cups (85g) shredded coconut

1 Combine coconut cream, rinds and chocolate in small saucepan; stir over low heat until smooth. Transfer mixture to small bowl, cover; refrigerate 3 hours or overnight.

2 Line baking tray with baking parchment. Working with a quarter of the chocolate mixture at a time (keeping remainder in refrigerator), roll rounded teaspoons into balls; place on tray. Refrigerate truffles until firm.

3 Working quickly, roll truffles in coconut, return to tray; refrigerate until firm.

white chocolate crackles

preparation time 10 minutes (plus refrigeration time) makes 24

1 cup (35g) Rice Krispies
1 cup (35g) Coco Pops
2 x 35g tubes mini M&Ms
200g white eating chocolate, melted

1 Line two 12-hole (1 tablespoon/20ml) mini muffin trays with paper cases.

2 Combine ingredients in medium bowl. Divide mixture among prepared holes, cover; refrigerate 10 minutes.

4 x 60g Snickers bars, chopped coarsely
1 cup (35g) Rice Krispies
150g toasted marshmallows, chopped coarsely
1 cup (140g) roasted unsalted peanuts
400g milk eating chocolate, chopped coarsely
2 teaspoons vegetable oil

snickers rocky road

preparation time 15 minutes   cooking time 3 minutes (plus refrigeration time)
makes 54

1 Grease 19cm x 29cm shallow cake tin. Line base and two long sides with baking parchment, extending parchment 2cm above sides of tin. Combine Snickers, Rice Krispies, marshmallows and nuts in large bowl.

2 Combine chocolate and oil in microwave-safe bowl; cook on medium-low (30%) in microwave oven for 1 minute. Using oven mitts, remove bowl from microwave oven; stir chocolate, return bowl to microwave oven. Repeat cooking and stirring until chocolate is melted; cool 5 minutes.

3 Pour chocolate mixture into Snickers mixture; mix until well combined. Spoon mixture into tin; refrigerate, covered, about 30 minutes or until set. Remove from tin, trim edges of mixture; cut into 3cm squares. Store rocky road, covered, in refrigerator.

chocolate nut clusters

preparation time 20 minutes cooking time 10 minutes
(plus refrigeration time) makes 24

¼ cup (35g) shelled unsalted
pistachios
¼ cup (35g) slivered almonds
150g milk eating chocolate,
chopped coarsely
½ cup (80g) sultanas

1 Line baking tray with baking parchment.

2 Heat small heavy-based frying pan; roast pistachios and almonds, stirring constantly, until browned lightly. (Take care; nuts burn easily.) Remove nuts from hot pan; cool.

3 Place chocolate in microwave-safe bowl; cook on medium-low (30%) in microwave oven for 1 minute. Using oven mitts, remove bowl from microwave oven; stir chocolate, return bowl to microwave oven. Repeat cooking and stirring until chocolate is melted.

4 Stir nuts and sultanas into chocolate.

5 Use a teaspoon to scoop out heaped spoonfuls of chocolate mixture; place onto tray. Refrigerate, uncovered, until chocolate is completely set.

tips Coconut ice can be made one week ahead; store, in an airtight container, in the refrigerator.
★ Slice can be made three days ahead; store, in an airtight container, in the refrigerator.

hedgehog slice

preparation time 10 minutes (plus refrigeration time)
cooking time 5 minutes makes 18

¾ cup (180ml) sweetened
condensed milk
60g butter
125g dark eating chocolate,
chopped coarsely
125g plain sweet biscuits
⅓ cup (50g) unsalted roasted
peanuts
⅓ cup (55g) sultanas

1 Grease 8cm x 26cm shallow cake tin; line base and long sides with baking parchment, extending parchment 5cm above edges.

2 Combine condensed milk and butter in small saucepan; stir over low heat until smooth. Remove from heat, add chocolate; stir until smooth.

3 Break biscuits into small pieces in a large bowl. Add nuts and sultanas; stir in the chocolate mixture.

4 Spread mixture into tin; refrigerate 3 hours or until firm. Remove from tin before slicing.

coconut ice

preparation time 15 minutes (plus refrigeration time) makes 36

3½ cups (560g) icing sugar
2½ cups (200g) desiccated coconut
395g can sweetened condensed milk
1 teaspoon vanilla extract
pink food colouring

1 Line base and sides of greased deep 19cm-square cake tin with baking parchment.

2 Sift icing sugar into large bowl. Stir in coconut, condensed milk and extract.

3 Press half the mixture firmly over base of tin. Work colouring into remaining mixture; press evenly over white layer.

4 Refrigerate about 3 hours or until firm before cutting into squares.

glossary

all-bran a low-fat, high-fibre breakfast cereal based on wheat bran.

almonds flat, pointy ended nuts with pitted brown shell enclosing a creamy white kernel that is covered by a brown skin.

blanched brown skins removed.

flaked paper-thin slices.

ground nuts are powdered to a coarse flour texture for use in baking.

slivered small pieces cut lengthways.

slivered almonds

American-style pork ribs well-trimmed mid-loin ribs.

bacon rashers also known as slices of bacon, made from pork side, cured and smoked.

bagel small ring-shaped bread roll with a dense, chewy texture and shiny crust.

barbecue sauce a spicy, tomato-based sauce used to marinate, baste or as an accompaniment to meats.

basil we used sweet basil in our recipes, unless otherwise specified.

beef minute steak thin slices of beef topside or silverside.

beetroot also known as red beets; firm, round root vegetable.

bicarbonate of soda also known as baking soda.

breadcrumbs

stale one- or two-day-old bread made into crumbs by grating, blending or processing.

packaged fine-textured, crunchy, purchased white breadcrumbs.

butter use salted or unsalted butter; 125g is equal to 1 stick butter.

buttermilk sold alongside fresh milk products in supermarkets and is commercially made by a method similar to yoghurt. Despite the implication of its name, it is low in fat and is a good substitute for dairy products such as cream or soured cream.

cabanossi a ready-to-eat Polish sausage; also known as cabana.

cayenne pepper a thin-fleshed, long, extremely hot dried red chilli, usually purchased ground.

cheese

cheddar the most common cow-milk 'tasty' cheese; should be aged, hard and have a pronounced bite.

beetroot

cream cheese commonly known as Philadelphia, a soft cow-milk cheese.

mozzarella soft, spun-curd cheese; originated in southern Italy where it is traditionally made from water buffalo milk. It has a low melting point and wonderfully elastic texture when heated, and is used to add texture rather than flavour.

mozzarella

parmesan also known as parmigiano, parmesan is a hard, grainy cow-milk cheese that originated in the Parma region of Italy. The curd is salted in brine for a month before being aged for up to two years in humid conditions.

pizza cheese a commercial blend of varying proportions of processed grated mozzarella, cheddar and parmesan.

ricotta soft white cow-milk cheese; roughly translates as "cooked again". It's made from whey, a by-product of other cheese making, to which fresh milk and acid are added. Ricotta is a sweet, moist cheese with a fat content of around 8.5% and a slightly grainy texture.

chives related to the onion and leek; has a subtle onion flavour.

chorizo sausage a sausage of Spanish origin, made of coarsely ground pork and highly seasoned with garlic and chillies.

cocoa powder also known as cocoa; dried, unsweetened, roasted then ground cocoa beans.

coconut

cream is obtained commercially from the first pressing of the coconut flesh alone, without the addition of water; the second pressing (less rich) is sold as the milk. Available in cans and cartons at supermarkets.

desiccated unsweetened, dried, concentrated and finely shredded coconut flesh.

shredded thin strips of dried coconut.

coriander also known as cilantro or Chinese parsley; bright-green-leafed herb with a pungent flavour.

coriander

corn chips packaged snack food that evolved from fried corn tortilla pieces.

cornflakes crisp flakes of corn.

cream

soured a thick, cultured soured cream.

whipping a cream which has a thickener.

custard powder instant mixture used to make pouring custard.

custard, prepared pouring custard, available in cartons.

extract just as the word means, an extract is made by actually extracting the flavour from a food product. In the case of vanilla, pods are soaked, usually in alcohol, to capture the authentic flavour.

flour

plain an all-purpose flour, made from wheat.

self-raising plain flour that has been sifted with baking powder in the proportion of 1 cup plain flour to 2 teaspoons baking powder.

gelatine we used powdered gelatine; also available in sheet form known as leaf gelatine.

ginger when fresh is also known as green or root ginger; the thick gnarled root of a tropical plant. Ground ginger is used as a flavouring in cakes, pies and puddings and cannot be substituted for fresh ginger.

golden syrup a by-product of refined sugarcane; pure maple syrup or honey can be substituted.

hummus a Middle-Eastern dip made from softened dried chickpeas, garlic, lemon juice and tahini (sesame seed paste); can be purchased, ready-made, from most delicatessens, supermarkets and health food stores.

hundreds and thousands tiny sugar-syrup-coated sugar crystals that come in a variety of bright colours. Used to decorate cakes and desserts.

instant pudding mix a blancmange-style (sweet pudding made with milk) dessert mix.

jam also known as preserve or conserve; most often made from fruit.

jelly crystals an instant mixture of powdered gelatine, granulated sugar, flavouring and colouring.

kiwi fruit also known as Chinese gooseberry.

lamb, French-trimmed cutlet rack all the fat and gristle at the narrow end of the bone have been removed.

malted milk powder instant powdered product made from cow milk and extracts of malted barley and other cereals.

maple syrup a thin syrup distilled from the sap of the maple tree. Maple-flavoured syrup or pancake syrup is not an adequate substitute for the real thing.

marmalade a preserve, usually based on citrus fruit.

mayonnaise we prefer to use whole egg mayonnaise in our recipes.

mexibeans a canned mix of red kidney beans, capsicum, tomato and spices.

minced meat also known as ground meat, as in beef, pork, lamb, veal and chicken.

mixed dried fruit a combination of sultanas, raisins, currants, mixed peel and cherries.

mixed spice a blend of ground spices usually consisting of cinnamon, allspice and nutmeg.

muesli also known as granola, a combination of grains (mainly oats), nuts and dried fruits. Some manufacturers toast their product in oil and honey, adding crispness and kilojoules.

mushrooms, button small, cultivated white mushrooms with a mild flavour.

button mushrooms

mustard

dijon a pale brown, distinctively flavoured fairly mild French mustard.

powder finely ground white (yellow) mustard seeds.

wholegrain also known as seeded. A French-style coarse-grain mustard made from crushed mustard seeds and dijon-style French mustard.

nutella chocolate hazelnut spread.

nutmeg the dried nut of an evergreen tree native to Indonesia; it is available in ground form or you can grate your own with a fine grater.

oil

cooking spray we use a cholesterol-free cooking oil spray made from canola oil.

olive made from ripened olives. Extra virgin and virgin olive oil are the first and second press, respectively, of the olives and considered the best. Extra light or light olive oil is diluted and refers to taste not fat levels.

groundnut pressed from ground peanuts; most commonly used oil in Asian cooking because of its high smoke point (capacity to handle high heat without burning).

sesame made from roasted, crushed white sesame seeds; a flavouring rather than a cooking medium.

vegetable oils sourced from plants rather than animal fats.

onion

spring also known as scallion; an immature onion picked before the bulb has formed, having a long, bright-green edible stalk.

spring onion and red onion

red also known as red Spanish, Spanish or Bermuda onion; a large, sweet-flavoured, purple-red onion.

paprika ground dried red pepper, available sweet or hot.

parsley, flat-leaf a flat-leaf variety of parsley also known as Italian parsley or continental parsley.

flat-leaf parsley

peanut butter peanuts ground to a paste; available as crunchy or smooth.

pepper also known as capsicum. They can be red, green, yellow, orange or purplish black. Seeds and membranes should be discarded before use.

peppers

pide also known as Turkish bread, comes in long (about 45cm) flat loaves as well as individual rounds.

pine nuts also known as pignoli; not a nut, but a small, cream-coloured kernel from pine cones.

pistachio delicately flavoured, pale green nut with a hard shell. To peel, soak shelled nuts in boiling water for about 5 minutes; drain, then pat dry with absorbent paper. Rub skins with cloth to peel.

pitta wheat-flour pocket bread is sold in large, flat pieces that easily separate into two thin rounds. Also available in small thick pieces called pocket pitta.

pizza bases pre-packaged for home-made pizzas. They come in a variety of sizes (snack or family) and thicknesses (thin and crispy or thick).

plain cake crumbs made from plain uniced cake.

polenta also known as cornmeal; a flour-like cereal made of dried corn (maize), sold ground in several different textures; also the name of the dish made from it.

prosciutto cured, air-dried (unsmoked), pressed ham; usually sold thinly sliced.

puff pastry, ready-rolled packaged sheets of frozen puff pastry, available from supermarkets.

rice, long-grain elongated grains that remain separate when cooked; most popular steaming rice in Asia.

rocket also known as arugula, rugula and rucola; a peppery-tasting green leaf that can be used similarly to baby spinach leaves, eaten raw in salads or used in cooking. Baby rocket leaves are both smaller and less peppery.

rocket

rolled oats also known as porridge; these are flattened oat grains rolled into flakes.

salami cured (air-dried) sausage heavily seasoned with garlic and spices.

salsa Spanish for sauce; a combination of tomatoes, onions, capsicums, vinegar, herbs and spices.

Snickers bar made from chocolate, peanuts, glucose, sugar, milk powder, butter and egg white.

Swiss chard also known as silver beet or chard; a leafy, dark green vegetable, related to the beet, with thick, crisp white or red stems and ribs.

soy sauce also known as sieu; is made from fermented soy beans.

spinach

spinach also known as English spinach. Tender green leaves are good uncooked in salads or added to soups, stir-fries and stews just before serving.

stock available in cans, bottles or tetra packs. Stock cubes or powder can be used.

stock cube

sugar

brown an extremely soft, fine granulated sugar retaining molasses for its characteristic colour and flavour.

caster also known as superfine or finely granulated table sugar.

sugar

icing also known as confectioners' sugar or powdered sugar.

white granulated table sugar, also known as crystal sugar.

sultanas also known as golden raisins; dried seedless white grapes.

sweet chilli sauce mild, Thai sauce made from red chillies, sugar, garlic and vinegar.

sweetened condensed milk from which 60% of the water has been removed; the remaining milk is then sweetened with sugar.

taco seasoning a packaged seasoning meant to duplicate the Mexican sauce made from oregano, cumin, chillies and other spices.

taco seasoning

tomato

canned whole peeled tomatoes in natural juices.

cherry also known as tiny tim or tom thumb tomatoes, small and round.

paste triple-concentrated tomato puree used to flavour soups, stews, sauces and casseroles.

plum also called egg or roma; these are smallish, oval-shaped tomatoes much used in Italian cooking or salads.

plum tomato

sauce also known as ketchup.

semi-dried partially dried tomato pieces in olive oil; softer and juicer than sun-dried, but do not keep as long.

vinegar, balsamic originally from Modena, Italy; there are now many balsamic vinegars on the market ranging in pungency and quality depending on how, and how long, they have been aged. Quality can be determined up to a point by price; use the most expensive sparingly.

worcestershire sauce a dark-brown, thin, spicy sauce used as a seasoning for meat, gravies and cocktails and as a condiment.

index

conversion charts

measuring equipment

The cup and spoon measurements used in this book are metric: one measuring cup holds approximately 250ml; one metric tablespoon holds 20ml; one metric teaspoon holds 5ml.

how to measure

The most accurate way of measuring dry ingredients is to weigh them. When using graduated metric measuring cups, shake dry ingredients loosely into the appropriate cup. Do not tap the cup on a bench or tightly pack the ingredients unless directed to do so. Level top of measuring cups and spoons with a knife. When measuring liquids, place a clear glass or plastic jug with metric markings on a flat surface to check accuracy at eye level.
We use large eggs having an average weight of 60g.

warning This book may contain recipes for dishes made with raw or lightly cooked eggs. These should be avoided by vulnerable people such as pregnant and nursing mothers, invalids, the elderly, babies and young children.

dry measures

METRIC	IMPERIAL
15g	½oz
30g	1oz
60g	2oz
90g	3oz
125g	4oz (¼lb)
155g	5oz
185g	6oz
220g	7oz
250g	8oz (½lb)
280g	9oz
315g	10oz
345g	11oz
375g	12oz (¾lb)
410g	13oz
440g	14oz
470g	15oz
500g	16oz (1lb)
750g	24oz (1½lb)
1kg	32oz (2lb)

liquid measures

METRIC	IMPERIAL
30ml	1 fluid oz
60ml	2 fluid oz
100ml	3 fluid oz
125ml	4 fluid oz
150ml	5 fluid oz (¼ pint/1 gill)
190ml	6 fluid oz
250ml	8 fluid oz
300ml	10 fluid oz (½ pint)
500ml	16 fluid oz
600ml	20 fluid oz (1 pint)
1000ml (1 litre)	1¾ pints

length measures

METRIC	IMPERIAL
3mm	⅛in
6mm	¼in
1cm	½in
2cm	¾in
2.5cm	1in
5cm	2in
6cm	2½in
8cm	3in
10cm	4in
13cm	5in
15cm	6in
18cm	7in
20cm	8in
23cm	9in
25cm	10in
28cm	11in
30cm	12in (1ft)

oven temperatures

These oven temperatures are only a guide for conventional ovens.
For fan-forced ovens, check the manufacturer's manual.

	°C (CELSIUS)	°F (FAHRENHEIT)	GAS MARK
Very low	120	250	½
Low	150	275-300	1-2
Moderately low	170	325	3
Moderate	180	350-375	4-5
Moderately hot	200	400	6
Hot	220	425-450	7-8
Very hot	240	475	9

ACP Books
General manager Christine Whiston
Test kitchen food director Pamela Clark
Editorial director Susan Tomnay
Creative director Hieu Chi Nguyen
Director of sales Brian Cearnes
Marketing manager Bridget Cody
Business analyst Rebecca Varela
Operations manager David Scotto
International rights enquiries Laura Bamford
lbamford@acpuk.com

ACP Books are published by ACP Magazines a division of PBL Media Pty Limited

Group publisher, Women's lifestyle Pat Ingram
Director of sales, Women's lifestyle Lynette Phillips
Commercial manager, Women's lifestyle Seymour Cohen
Marketing director, Women's lifestyle Matthew Dominello
Public relations manager, Women's lifestyle Hannah Deveraux
Creative director, Events, Women's lifestyle Luke Bonnano
Research Director, Women's lifestyle Justin Stone
ACP Magazines, Chief Executive officer Scott Lorson
PBL Media, Chief Executive officer Ian Law

Produced by ACP Books, Sydney.
Published by ACP Books, a division of ACP Magazines Ltd, 54 Park St, Sydney; GPO Box 4088, Sydney, NSW 2001.
phone (02) 9282 8618 fax (02) 9267 9438.
acpbooks@acpmagazines.com.au
www.acpbooks.com.au
Printed and bound in China.

Australia Distributed by Network Services,
phone +61 2 9282 8777 fax +61 2 9264 0278
networkweb@networkservicescompany.com.au
United Kingdom Distributed by Australian Consolidated Press (UK),
phone (01604) 642 200 fax (01604) 642 300 books@acpuk.com
New Zealand Distributed by Netlink Distribution Company,
phone (9) 366 9966 ask@ndc.co.nz
South Africa Distributed by PSD Promotions,
phone (27 11) 392 6065/6/7 fax (27 11) 392 6079/80
orders@psdprom.co.za
Canada Distributed by Publishers Group Canada
phone (800) 663 5714 fax (800) 565 3770 service@raincoast.com

A catalogue record for this book is available from the British Library.
ISBN 978-1-903777-39-8
© ACP Magazines Ltd 2008
ABN 18 053 273 546
This publication is copyright. No part of it may be reproduced or transmitted in any form without the written permission of the publishers.